# GREAT STORE PERFORMANCE:

## FROM ILLUSION TO REALITY

## THOMAS RISKAS

Bloomington, IN  Milton Keynes, UK

authorHOUSE

*AuthorHouse™*
*1663 Liberty Drive, Suite 200*
*Bloomington, IN 47403*
*www.authorhouse.com*
*Phone: 1-800-839-8640*

*AuthorHouse™ UK Ltd.*
*500 Avebury Boulevard*
*Central Milton Keynes, MK9 2BE*
*www.authorhouse.co.uk*
*Phone: 08001974150*

*First published by AuthorHouse 9/5/2006*

*ISBN: 1-4259-3535-4 (sc)*
*ISBN: 1-4259-3534-6 (dj)*

*Library of Congress Control Number: 2006904710*

*Printed in the United States of America*
*Bloomington, Indiana*

*This book is printed on acid-free paper.*

# CONTENTS

# ACKNOWLEDGEMENTS:

I feel deeply indebted to those who have played a significant role in this work.

My life companion, "chief collaborator," and best friend, Debbie, has provided insightful feedback and invaluable support to me, both personally and professionally. Her perspective has been grounding and thought–provoking, and her support has been sustaining and encouraging.

My long-time friend and colleague Alan Anderson, as well as Pat Weger, Barbara Grisby, Michael Ryan and Lori Sledge – have all contributed greatly to the integrity and substance of this work, providing much needed insight and wisdom.

Our retail clients deserve a special word of thanks. We are continually impressed by the dedication of the many retail stores' executives and managers we have worked with through the years.

To my executive reviewers, Larry Stone, Michael O'Dell, Jon Cannon, Larry Merlo, Donald Mierzwa, Mark Giresi, Kathy Self, Bob Povirk, Mark Thienes, Karl Dixon, Gil Mohesky, Gary Marshall, John Ortiz, Steve Davis, Dan Caspersen, Patricia Dirks, Dave Eske, Bob Colgrove, Neal Stacey, Bob Thompson, Mark Hasting, Kristi Broadwater, and George Lutzow: Your feedback and suggestions were indispensable. Thank you for taking time out of your busy schedules to read and review this book.

I will always owe a special debt of gratitude to my friends, Julius Jones and Dan Caspersen, previously with Target Stores, who initiated me into the retail sector and made me an integral part of the leadership team in Region 200 for nearly seven years.

Finally, I want to thank Linda Cashdan for her invaluable editorial assistance and Jessica Murphy for her keen eye and expertise in proofreading.

# PREFACE:

This book addresses the unique challenges of multi- unit retail field leadership, focusing specifically on the problem of inconsistent store performance and the goal of achieving great store performance. In this Preface, I would like to provide some essential background information as the context for what follows in the remaining pages.

Several years ago, I was asked by a large chain retailer to find a way to ensure more consistent results and development in their stores by working in their various Divisions with the Division Presidents and their Regional Vice Presidents (RVPs) and District Managers (DMs). Specifically, this organization, like all the others we have researched and worked with subsequently, was troubled by inconsistent store performance and wanted to better understand what was underneath that inconsistency and how to deal with it. Additionally, it was rightly suspected that class room training and other traditional forms of leadership development, though important, were insufficient in developing leaders in the area of field leadership. Their RVPs, DMs and Store Managers (SMs) knew from experience what it took to run a successful store that was brand consistent, customer focused and operationally sound. Knowledge, experience and the desire to do a good job were not missing. The problem was not about retail competence, desire or hard work. Nor was it about lack of standards or excessive turnover, although turnover and team instability were certainly symptoms.

Accordingly, I was commissioned to go into the field and observe how the RVPs -and DMs were managing in the field as they visited stores to assess and improve store performance through their interactions with SMs and other executives and associates in the stores.

The difficulty, it turned out, involved two primary areas of concern. As a relevant aside, we have found these same two areas of concern in every other chain store retail organization we have worked with over the past nearly two decades. This company was no exception and it is likely that even your organization, given the rather "incestuous" quality of the retail sector, would suffer from the same or similar challenges.

The first area of difficulty I discovered was seated at the highest level of the organization in the structural confusion between centralized store support functions and the stores line organization. The thinking shared by many CEOs in the retail sector that it is possible to compete effectively on the basis of brand consistency and customer shopping experience is ironically and clearly undermined by the confused stewardships and accountabilities associated with centralized store support infra-structures.

This, in my experience, is a serious dilemma confronting CEOs and senior executives in numerous chain store companies today and one that I have addressed in some depth in Chapter 5 of this book. We have found that this dilemma consistently undermines brand integrity and makes the vision of "great store performance" more of an illusion than a reality.

The second area of difficulty undermining consistently effective store performance in this particular organization, and others we have worked with since, was in a deeply inbred retail-management "store visit" approach used by RVPs and DMs to inspect and improve store conditions and performance. This approach, we found, severely undermined empowerment, accountability and team performance and development within the stores and resulted in the recurrence of certain common problems as well as service and operational blindness, i.e. a failure to see and attend to obvious needs, or deficiencies, and exploit opportunities for improvement. In short, the research showed that regional and district executives in the field were inadvertently contributing to inconsistent store performance, contrary to their best intentions.

This understanding provided important answers to the questions that had haunted this retailer for years, i.e., given that the store executives know what is required to run a successful store, why are store performance and results so inconsistent and why do they keep addressing the same problems again and again? As it turns out these questions haunt every senior retail executive we've worked with over the years since then and inspired both the design of the field coaching approach we currently use and the writing of the book.

Our work and this book are the product of field research involving the observation of thousands of field executives in over a thousand store visits with VPs and DMs who have worked with various other major retailers, including Target Corp., Albertsons, Safeway, Kroger, OSCO, CVS, PetsMart, Office-Max, Circuit City, Best Buy, Mervyn's and others. The results have been telling, showing that, at best, the way field VPs and DMs "visit" stores and manage store performance can only lead to minimal compliance, not to consistent performance, accountability or commitment. According to our field research, experienced VPs and DMs, through what we refer to as the 'inspect/ direct/correct' approach to field leadership, consistently and defensively focus on the wrong problems without effectively addressing the real reasons why brand and performance standards are not being consistently met, why the execution of strategic change is deficient or inconsistent, why turnover is so high ( or, in some cases, not high enough), why obvious opportunities for improvement are being missed or why associates or team members in the stores are not changing, improving or, in many cases, thinking beyond rote habit or provided direction.

Essentially, through the conventional approach of retail management during store visits, field VPs and DMs inspect store conditions, point-out problems or opportunities (others should have seen but missed), direct others to a solution (that was already known but not addressed or applied) to establish or restore a level of compliance to known standards that were either never fully attained or once attained but lost. This approach of field leadership not only creates an anti learning environment and a dependent store management team, it also undermines engagement and accountability at the store level and reduces the VP and DM to auditors and de-facto Store Managers, reducing Store Managers in turn to mere operators and raising the question of why three layers of management are needed to essentially do the same thing.

The passion for this book comes from my quest to understand how we learn and change, and how leaders can create the conditions for empowerment, accountability, and internal commitment in the workplace. Although I have consulted with many organizations in various industries, my work in recent years has been concentrated in the retail sector. For that reason I have chosen retail field management as my primary research focus.

I have done so, in part, because of the positive experiences I've had with the dedicated men and women I have coached in this sector. I have found so many of them to be humble, receptive to learning, and easy to relate to.

Another reason for my choice is the opportunity to make a significant impact. As I see it, the development of retail field executives has been relatively neglected. Although many companies offer training programs, most are defensively oriented and ineffectual, resulting in management routines that cause more problems than they solve.

This is not only true in retail. In every sector I have worked in over the span of my career, management's professed desire for developmental leadership and the related ideals of empowerment, accountability, stewardship, and internal commitment, have been well intentioned illusions at best, what Chris Argyris of Harvard referred to as "the Emperor's new clothes."

As a result, the meaning and implications of the research findings and conclusions presented herein, although focused on the retail sector, pertain to leadership in any domain. As one reviewer put it, what's contained in this book is "something every leader must know to achieve superior results."

ThomasRiskas
Las Vegas, NV

# INTRODUCTION:

# QUESTIONS AND DILEMMAS

What is "great store performance"? Why is it desirable? Is great store performance an illusion or a reality? If it's a reality, then why is it so elusive, and what can be done to achieve it?

In this Introduction I will provide a foundational answer to the first question and overview answers to the remaining three. All four will be addressed in greater depth throughout the book.

The term "store" means different things to different people. For some, a store is a catalogue. For others, it is a kiosk in a shopping mall. For yet others, it is a website. In this book "store" means a *brick and mortar establishment* operating within a larger retail organization that sells services and/or products to customers or patrons.

At its most basic level, the store is a place of business, a company profit center. However, it is also a place of relationship and exchange between the company and its customers, and a showcase for the best the company has to offer. It's a reflection of the company's uniqueness and value, its "brand promise."

*Great store performance*, as used in this book, is a vision that encompasses all those different characteristics. As a business unit of the corporation, *great store performance* translates into financial results that are consistently at or above plan. More specifically, it refers to stores that consistently perform at or above plan in *every* department or performance category, month after month. This definition, by necessity, assumes a relatively intact store team and relatively stable local market conditions for the determined periods of time.

By "relatively intact store team," we mean that the same store manager and at least 70% of the store team are in place for the periods in question. By "relatively stable local market conditions," we mean that there are no unusual circumstances negatively affecting shopping activity and consumer spending for the periods in question. The "periods in question" need to be of sufficient duration to attribute results to the incumbent store manager and team.

Broadening these qualifiers would provide undeserved praise and comfort to mediocre-to-good store teams and field executives and make the idea of great store performance a non-starter. On the other hand, great store teams rarely, if ever, take comfort in past performance and do not need praise or recognition to inspire their commitment to excellence. Success is its own reward.

In terms of the company's brand promise to its customers, *great store performance* means operational excellence and world-class service. The company's "brand promise" might include such factors as price, value, selection, service, quality, and conditions throughout every part of the store that shape and define the entire shopping experience.

All of this suggests that the ideal of "greatness," or world-class store performance, as we define it, is not determined by an isolated category or department "comps," "run rates," average period results, single period results, single or cluster category results, or overall store performance. Nor is it defined by team "spirit," morale or enthusiasm. In a world-class store, *every* aspect of store performance, especially those affecting the customers' shopping experience, excels consistently, month after month. The store team is consistently "firing on all eight cylinders."

Why is great store performance necessary or desirable? For some retail leaders, intense competition and changing shopping patterns have created a radical rethinking of strategic focus. This has resulted in a fundamental shift from the traditional emphasis on the 4-Ps of the "marketing-mix" (product, price, promotion, place) to a focus instead on the overall shopping experience.

To others, however, something less than great store performance, as we define it, is perfectly acceptable. We certainly can't argue against this position since many retailers have been very successful financially by achieving something far less than great store performance.

We, however, see the store as the primary, if not exclusive, result-producing area of the business. This is where the company meets the customer and therefore the competition. As a result, store performance is the first line of defense against market erosion by the competition and the primary determinant of competitive advantage.

We are frankly unimpressed by the size and reputation of the "big-box" retail chains that dominate the market on the basis of "everyday low prices." In our experience, size, and the hubris that comes with it, covers a multitude of managerial and organizational "sins" that eventually take their toll on company growth, profitability, customer service and employee satisfaction. For retail companies committed to market leadership, operational excellence and consistent profit margins, great store performance is not an option or a luxury. It is a necessity.

Assuming its desirability, is great store performance achievable, or is it merely an illusion?

Perhaps both. It's an illusion in that we have yet to witness it in any of the major retailers we have researched. However, we know the goal is achievable in both theory and practice because we have seen such "greatness" in many stores we have worked with over time. Companies that achieve great store performance do so by making and sustaining recommended changes in at least three critical areas: leadership roles and focus, developmental focus and approach, and orientation to leadership action.

**Leadership roles and focus**: We think great store performance requires a radical change in the role of store manager. The move toward centralized store support has transformed the store manager into a cost center manager who functions as a custodian and operator of the store. We argue this reduces his management role and severely limits store performance.

To attain great store performance, the store manager role needs to change dramatically, functioning essentially as an empowered General Manager (GM) with full P&L responsibility for the store, with all that such implies. Additionally, the focus of the store manager as "leader" needs to shift from control-based supervision to "development" through the consistent application of what we term in Chapter 3 as the missing "Leadership Factor." This shift in focus makes the continual building and upgrading of the store team the store manager's primary emphasis and top priority.

In addition, we frame the relationship between the store manager and the next level of management as a "partnership" rather than as a traditional boss/subordinate relationship. We think great store performance depends primarily on an empowered, engaged, and accountable store manager.

As suggested in Chapter 2, this has serious implications for the caliber of person retained to function as a store manager. It also has serious implications on the roles of other field executives, notably the Vice Presidents (VPs) and District Managers (DMs). These executive roles, which have been reduced to bureaucratic administrators and compliance auditors, are functioning as de-facto store managers – "super store managers." We argue that these roles also need to change, that the leader of each level of the hierarchy in the store's organization should function as a GM and 'developmental' leader of his or her respective team and as either managing or reporting partners with their respective direct reports and managers.

Finally, the change in leadership roles has profound implications on the stewardship of the various "store support" functions of the business. In Chapter 5 we address these and challenge the CEO and senior executives to wrestle with the tensions between the stores and the corporate, divisional, and regional store support functions. We present several questions demanding attention and resolution through dialogue.

We contend that to achieve the vision of great store performance a very different relationship between the stores and the store support functions is needed. Instead of functioning as "customers" of the stores, store support "staff" should operate as "suppliers" and "advisors" to the "line" managers (or GMs) of the stores, supplying resources and information and providing expert advice as needed.

This means that neither store support executives and directors nor line field executives would dictate policy and programs to the stores. It also means, as implied in Chapters 3 and 5, that necessary brand consistency, decision support and economies of scale be realized through the "performance partnership agreements" (or PPAs) established between and among the various levels of the "line" organization.

Essentially, it will become clear by the end of Chapter 5 that we advocate a "partnering organization" based on the principle of "stewardship." Such an organizational paradigm would transcend and embrace the best of both centralized and decentralized worlds.

**Developmental focus and approach:** Our vision for development involves the three fundamentals of effective execution - empowerment, accountability and learning. These three fundamentals, which in this book differ significantly in meaning from common understandings, comprise what we see as a missing leadership factor. The application of this essential leadership factor through continual developmental store performance interventions (or "store visits") constitutes what we refer to as the developmental focus and approach of field leadership. We present and apply this approach in Chapters 3 and 5 respectively.

**Orientation to leadership action**: We propose a personal and cultural transition from a defensive orientation to action to a collaborative orientation to action. A defensive orientation, presented in Chapter 4, bases decision-making and store performance on control-based approaches to field leadership and store management. A collaborative orientation, presented in Chapter 5, optimizes decision-making and store performance through partnering, learning and problem solving.

As we see it, the above three required areas of change are clearly interrelated and essential. With a genuine, long-term commitment to all three areas, the vision of great store performance is achievable. Without it, the goal will remain an illusion.

Given the achievability of such a vision, how specifically can the elusiveness of great store performance be explained? To answer this question we turn to the findings of extensive action research conducted in various major retail organizations.

Over the past nearly two decades, we have observed over one thousand retail store visits in a variety of retail organizations including Target Stores, Mervyn's, PetsMart, Office-Max, and Albertsons. These store visits, which again were managerial performance-improvement interventions, involved thousands of field executives and store managers who were in pursuit of more effective and consistent store performance.

Since many of those field executives had recently migrated from other companies, we gained valuable insight into the field management routines of numerous other major retailers as well, including Wal-Mart, K-Mart, Best Buy, Safeway, CVS, Walgreens, Sears, Toys-R-Us, and others. When asked to compare current managerial practices with those of previous employers, newly or recently hired field executives confirmed that the processes and approach to field management were virtually identical.

Our research has discovered common, recurring problems in a wide variety of retail operations, large and small, be they grocery stores, specialty products and services stores, department stores, clothing stores, convenience stores or discount stores. Our research has also uncovered three vexing and puzzling dilemmas field executives consistently felt incapable of solving:

**DILEMMA #1:** "Given all the experience we have in our stores' organization, in our field executives, our store managers and the department managers within the stores, **why do we continue to experience the same problems over and over again?**"

Virtually all of these companies invested considerable resources in recruiting bright, capable, experienced managers. They developed and implemented extensive training programs for store management and field executives. They established highly detailed structures, systems, processes, policies and procedures for the effective management of the stores' organization.

In all cases, we were dealing with field executives, including Division Presidents, Regional or Territory VPs and District Managers, who had worked in retail management for many years, many of them with experience at multiple companies. Yet, the problems they all faced on a day-to-day basis were the very same problems they had been addressing throughout their careers.

The problems are not new. The solutions are not complicated, and they have all been addressed numerous times, often with the same store managers. So why do they continue to recur? *Why do we continue to address the same problems, with the same people, who are experienced and knowledgeable, over and over again?*

**DILEMMA #2:** What makes a store that has performed consistently, meeting its targets for several months, suddenly start under performing and missing plan? Or, as a variation of the same issue, how is it that a store can perform well one month, poorly the next month, then well again two months later? In other words, *why are we continuing to experience inconsistent performance and results? Why isn't good performance sustainable?*

In our experience, any region or district is only as good as its inconsistently performing stores and any store is only as good as its inconsistently performing department. This is a humbling idea that should give even well performing stores, districts and regions pause for reflection.

In spite of their best efforts and an intense focus on brand integrity and bottom-line performance, all of the retail organizations we've worked with face this dilemma of inconsistent performance. Good performing stores today, which as Jim Collins would suggest, are the enemy of "great" performing stores, could become marginal or poor performing stores tomorrow or simply remain "good" as a deterrent to greatness. This is a common problem. A particular store could be performing very well for months or even a year or two, and then, out of nowhere, for no apparent reason, its performance might begin to slide in one or more category. In most cases stores perform below standard and plan in more than one category every week of every month, and improvements are often short lived. This makes inconsistent performance one of the biggest challenges retail executives face on an ongoing basis.

Some regional executives with large enough territories are able to mask this problem from corporate management by playing the numbers. They know a certain number of stores will be down in a given period and certain other stores will be up. And they know their numbers and their stores well enough to be able to accurately predict a likely average, or bottom line, for their region. Effectiveness, in this case, means "playing the averages" and performing at or above "comps" in a given period. The law of compensatory and comparative performance is the rule in many cases. Net gains in operating and financial metrics are compared with other periods and other districts and regions to determine the level or quality of store performance.

Some retail executives use performance "run rates" to statistically project large financial gains on the basis of seasonally adjusted extrapolations of short-term improvements. This is a common defensive routine. The favorable "run rate" is often falsely attributed to applied "best practices" where no actual causal connection exists between the two, or to the harvest of low hanging fruit in broken stores. In either case, the use of such favorable run rates as an explanation for good performance is part of the defensive reasoning.

One Regional Vice President (RVP) we worked with was touted by corporate management as having an extraordinary ability to achieve targeted results consistently in his stores, month after month. Naturally, we were eager to validate this assessment and, if true, study his methods.

His secret? "It's all in the numbers," he told us. He readily admitted that he could no more predict performance at a specific store in a given month than he could predict the weather. But he knew his region extremely well. He could predict, plus or minus two or three points, what his region would produce in a given month, based largely upon history. He would focus his time and energy on harvesting the low hanging fruit, improving by a point here or there in certain categories, within certain stores, by manipulating hours or shifting inventory, all without systemically improving performance. He was also experienced enough to know that plus two or three points was always preferable to minus, or even getting lucky enough to hit the numbers right on the nose. Almost miraculously, his region could be counted on for hitting its numbers, with a little to spare.

This RVP, held up by senior executives as among the best in the company at consistently producing targeted results *in his region*, was, in reality, anxious to learn from *us* how he might actually be able to generate more predictable and consistent results *at the individual store level* – a challenge he shared with every other Regional Vice President in his company. And indeed, with every retail field executive we have researched.

This dilemma haunts every thoughtful retail executive we have observed. *Why are we unable to consistently achieve targeted results?*

**DILEMMA #3:** Given the first dilemma of executives addressing the same problems over and over again, and the second one which has them struggling to consistently achieve targeted results, a seemingly obvious question comes to mind: **"Why are we persisting in managing and leading in a way that is producing undesirable results?"**

Executives who are struggling to achieve consistently effective ("great") levels of performance in their divisions, regions and districts and who are bogged down in addressing the same problems with the same people, day after day, are continuing to do things exactly the same way, as if doing more of the same, or doing more of it in a given week, is somehow going to make a difference.

We always ask field executives in these situations why they're continuing to do what they, themselves, have proven doesn't work. In many cases they think that if they aren't getting the results they need, they need to work harder at attending to detail in the stores. They need to visit more stores every day, as if merely seeing more store managers addressing the same problems, with the same people in a given day is somehow going to improve execution in a way that translates to the bottom line.

Often field executives in these situations have a tendency toward denial. "It's not my leadership that is the problem; the problem is with the store manager. That's where the mistakes are being made and repeated. That's where the problem lies."

In other words, rather than looking in the mirror and asking, "How might my approach to leading contribute to poor or inconsistent performance?" they continually point to other people, usually the store manager, who can't anticipate problems, who can't execute effectively, who is overwhelmed and who doesn't know his business well enough to be able to predict and achieve consistent results. Even if the store managers are part of the problem – and they often are – they are clearly not the whole problem and are too often merely symptomatic of the deeper "management" problem resting with their bosses' failure to effectively staff, develop and lead.

To justify this lack of introspection and personal responsibility, VPs and DMs typically fall back on the defensive beliefs that they're doing what they have been taught, what they know, what the company has told them to do. It is how they've been led. It's the only leadership model they have, and they don't know any better. Or, it's the safest approach to take, given the caliber of the store managers they're working with and the likely embarrassment that would occur should a corporate executive drop in on a surprise visit. As we will learn in Chapter 4, this kind of defensive reasoning tends to foster the skilled incompetence that produces the same unwanted results or fails to produce desired results.

Whether or not they take responsibility for the situation and confront their own skilled incompetence, most field executives are vexed by the question, *"Why are you continuing to manage and lead with an approach that you know isn't working?"*

## A UNIVERSAL APPROACH TO RETAIL FIELD LEADERSHIP

Does any of this sound familiar? Are these dilemmas a reality in your organization? Our experience would suggest that they probably are.

If so, you are far from unique. In fact, we have yet to find a *single* senior executive in *any* major retail organization who, when being completely honest, does not agree that the organization is perplexed by these three dilemmas.

The degree to which these dilemmas vex executives across the retail sector is staggering. We have discovered, through our analysis of volumes of store visit transcripts, that there is a remarkable consistency in the fundamental leadership approach field executives take, regardless of the company or their title or level of experience.

In Chapter 1, we will illustrate this prevailing theory of action, which we refer to as the Inspect/Direct/Correct (IDC) approach to improving store performance. This approach is applied in the various routines of field VPs and DMs as they conduct periodic store visits to manage and improve store performance in their districts, regions and divisions.

Even more remarkably, this prevailing approach to retail field management is not limited to the United States. A recent business article recounting the grand opening of the U.S. outlet of a large, foreign-based retailer went into great detail on how the CEO of this company flew into the country to walk the floor of that store prior to opening, using the same fundamental approach to management as every one of the domestic retailers we have observed.

## CROSS-POLLINATION

Acknowledging the need for a breakthrough in the way they're managing in the field, many retail leaders we have worked with have adopted the practice of hiring successful people from other retail companies in order to benefit from the "best practices" within the industry.

An executive from one of the largest retailers in the U.S. explained to me that such an approach was one of their core strategies. They hired talent from other retail organizations in order to bring in the best practices in the industry. The problem, according to the research, is that the prevailing approach to leadership is the same throughout the industry. Thus, the cross-pollination has resulted in the industry drawing in the same "best practices" from each other, over and over again. It is an incestuous phenomenon.

## ACTION SCIENCE: THE RESEARCH AND DESIGN OF PERFORMANCE IMPROVEMENT INTERVENTIONS

Our research in the area of retail field leadership is based upon a methodology known as Action Research, which is foundational in the field of Action Science. This field is itself a discipline with a long pedigree of renowned social scientists such as John Dewey and Kurt Lewin. Over the past nearly 50 years, it has been developed and made popular by the extensive work of Chris Argyris, Donald Schon and their colleagues and associates at Harvard University. (See *Action Science* by Argyris, Putnam and Smith, 1985, Jossey-Bass; *Theory in Practice* by Argyris and Schon, 1974, Jossey-Bass; *Knowledge for Action* by Argyris, 1993, Jossey-Bass and *Organizational Learning II* by Argyris and Schon, 1996, Addison-Wesley.)

Generally speaking, Action Science is "an inquiry into how (we) design and implement action in relation to one another" (Argyris). The purpose of such designed action is to accomplish objectives by solving complex performance problems. Through Action Science "we seek knowledge that will serve action" (Argyris), and with such knowledge we achieve more consistently effective performance and results.

We view Action Science as a discipline that requires us to question our typical or habitual ways of thinking, acting and interacting at work. As applied to retail field management, the process we use involves an executive and a certified coach. The coach observes the executive at work, and together they assess his actions and design new approaches to the issues he handles, which are then tested through practice. The results are studied, and the cycle of the executive's learning continues.

There are two unique aspects to applied Action Science in the field. One is the focus on the gap between the executive's *intended approach* in addressing a problem to achieve a particular objective and the *actual approach* used. And the second is the collaborative design of additional, more developmental approaches to problem solving, which constitute new learning.

The first step requires the researcher, as observer, to determine, up front, the approach the executive intends to use. In the case of understanding a retail field executive's general approach to visiting stores, for example, we would ask:

> ➤  *What is your goal when you visit stores?*

> ➤  *What are your intentions?*

> ➤  *Where is your focus in improving store performance? Why such a focus?*

> ➤  *What approach do you take in identifying and solving store performance problems?*

➤  *What does such an approach look like?*

➤  *Why such an approach?*

➤  *What factors determine your approach?*

➤  *How might your approach differ when these determining factors change from...(this) to...(that)? Can you provide some examples?*

➤  *How do your approaches relate to your goals and intentions?*

➤  *How do you typically determine whether or not your approach has resulted in the achievement of desired or intended outcomes?*

➤  *What kind of information do you produce and how do you test that information for validity?*

This is all designed to get the executive to articulate, in detail, what he wants to accomplish when he goes into that store, how specifically he intends to do it, what his approach looks like behaviorally, and the rationale for his approach.

This first step of mapping out the intended approach is crucial to the development process, because there is often an execution gap between what the executive says he does, or wants and intends to do, and what he actually does. The identification of this gap can serve to "unfreeze" the executive's mind-set and allow for necessary unlearning to take place.

Such unlearning essentially involves breaking what isn't working, or even (in the spirit of *Good to Great*) what is working, in order to build a better approach. Without unlearning (or letting go of) existing ineffective approaches, the new learning cannot occur. Instead, the executive remains trapped in reactive routines, which are automatically activated when he confronts situations similar to those he encountered in the past. This explains, in part, how it is that we can learn and embrace new ways of leading and then, under the pressure of the real world, fall back to our old, ineffective approaches.

New learning is unproductive if the existing patterns of conditioned response have not been broken. People become very skilled at defensively blocking out an awareness of how their own skilled approaches to management are producing unwanted results. In other words, an executive's "skilled unawareness" and "skilled incompetence," to use Chris

Argyris' terms, remain intact and operative. The person remains stuck in a deeply embedded experience loop, believing he is acting differently and effectively, even though he is not. In such cases the hard facts confirm that the appearance or experience of change is an illusion.

There are, of course other, more fundamental factors that help explain why our well planned change initiatives and interventions don't work, some of which will be presented in Chapter 4. However, the failure to break the cycles of skilled incompetence and progress from poor, average, or good to great store performance through systematic and continuous action research and design is significant as a cause of inconsistent performance.

## SOLVING THE 3 DILEMMAS

So let's return to where we started, with the 3 Dilemmas that so universally vex retail field executives and make great store performance so elusive.

> ➢  *Why are we experiencing recurring problems?*

> ➢  *Why are we consistently experiencing the inconsistent achievement of targeted results?*

> ➢  *Why are we persisting in doing what doesn't work?*

The good news is that there are solutions to these dilemmas. As you might imagine, the solutions are not simple and are not easy to execute. Unfortunately, as will be evident in Chapter 4, this is not merely a matter of, say, *capitalizing on strengths and managing around weaknesses*, being *principle centered*, practicing certain *habits of highly effective people*, invoking the engagement of the *head, heart and hands*, staying *positive*, or getting the right people *on the bus* and in the right roles.

Nor is it a matter of reading this or any other book and going out tomorrow to solve the recurring problems and more consistently achieve desired results. It will take a lot more than that. The pervasive orientation to action that has made these dilemmas so universal and so difficult to solve in the retail environment has evolved over generations. Overcoming that orientation will require a willingness to repeatedly look squarely in the mirror and confront the brutal facts that lie at the heart of the problem. This is sound advice that comes from Collins' research in *Good to Great* and which we endorse and repeatedly refer to throughout this book (Collins, J., "Good to Great", 2001, Harper Business).

Achieving great store performance requires a commitment to leading and managing differently from the way you have before. The three dilemmas can be solved and your stores can achieve greatness by more consistently achieving or exceeding targeted results, but not without a *radically* different orientation and approach to field leadership.

Such a radical change, as we shall see, is fraught with difficulty and riddled with wrong turns, bumpy roads and dead ends. No attempted intervention is exempt from the resistance and self-deception that sabotage this important work. That is why, in our experience, traditional forms of classroom-based leadership training and development have not resulted in sustainable change and consistent improvements. The same holds true for traditional forms of performance management, involving feedback, profiling and performance evaluations, and directive, motivational coaching.

The close, on-site involvement of qualified and experienced Action Science Coaches has been the linchpin of this recommended developmental work from its inception. The work presented and advocated in the chapters that follow is rigorous and collaborative in nature. It is not a do-it-yourself self-help project. It requires expert field coaching. Some direction for internal Action Science coaching is presented in Chapter 3. This direction comes in the form of a suggested coaching process designed for use by internal "peer coaches" who have been adequately trained and certified to facilitate reflective learning through applied Action Science. Neither the certification process nor the intricacies of proper coaching can be adequately conveyed by a book.

You will learn in reading this book the requirements for making the transition from good to great store performance in your district or region. Specifically, you will learn what to do to make reporting managers accountable, engaged and internally committed partners, and how to facilitate your partners' ongoing development through collaborative action learning and problem solving in the stores.

You will also learn how to detect the flawed advice of internal and external experts whose proposed solutions create new problems and make old problems worse. Finally, you will learn what's driving erratic and inconsistent performance in the stores, how and why your approach to field leadership might be inadvertently contributing to counterproductive behavior, and what's required to understand and overcome resistance to change.

In one obvious sense, this book is outside the CEO's domain, since it is operational rather than strategic in nature. However, the concerns addressed in this book and the vision of great store performance itself are of paramount strategic concern to the organization's success and well-being. Understanding the dynamics of store performance is crucial in structuring and managing centralized store support functions and has transferable benefits to other areas of organizational performance as well.

Accordingly, while this book is written to and for retail field executives in the store's organization, including Vice Presidents and District Managers who regularly visit stores and work with store managers and store teams to improve store performance, it is also written with other retail executives in mind, specifically the CEO, the COO or EVP of Stores Operations, Division Presidents and the other executive directors of the various store support functions. All of the above executives and managers are faced with the question of what they really want from their store managers and store support directors. More specifically, many of the following questions will be asked, implied and addressed:

Does management want stewards who are truly responsible and accountable for store performance and results, or 'hired hands' that function as operators, attendants, and supervisors?

Does management want store managers who function as GMs and profit center managers over their multi-million dollar operations, or as custodians and cost center managers?

What is management's vision of the role of store manager? What is management's vision of great store performance? What is management willing to pay for? What powers is management willing to release?

How does management want field executives to function? As suppliers of resources and facilitators of development to store managers, or as compliance auditors and de facto "super" store managers?

Does management want empowered, accountable and internally committed leaders and associates, or compliant employees who follow orders like good soldiers and go the extra mile to please the boss?

Finally, does management want great store performance as defined earlier, from many, if not most, of the stores, or is management content with the current level of store performance, which is likely mediocre-to-good at best?

Chances are, management says it wants great store performance, but is not doing what it has to do to get it. What is really wanted? This question, which we would suggest not be answered too quickly or definitively, is asked implicitly throughout the book and pointedly in Chapter 5 regarding the dilemma of centralized store support.

Our hope is that you, the reader, regardless of your title or role in the management hierarchy, will hold on to the tension in the above questions and those presented at the beginning of each chapter and throughout the book. Great store performance *is* achievable. Management must decide, after reading this book, what they really want and what they're willing to risk. If executives and managers find that they really want the vision of great store performance, then it stands to reason that its realization requires both sacrifice and risk, as all commitment does. Great store performance is not achieved easily or cheaply. That being said, let's proceed.

# CHAPTER 1

# THE PREVAILING APPROACH TO RETAIL FIELD MANAGEMENT: IS IT WORKING?

*In this chapter:*

➢ *What do field executives do very well that hurts store performance and results?*

➢ *Why is it so difficult for stores to achieve or exceed plan consistently?*

➢ *Why aren't store managers consistently anticipating and resolving obvious store problems without the need for inspections?*

How do field executives approach the objective of improving store performance? Many retail executives have insisted, before being observed in action, that the way they visit stores is very different from what the research describes as the "prevailing approach" of retail field leadership.

One District Manager (DM) we worked with saw himself as part of what he referred to as "the new breed" of DMs, which coaches more, asks more questions and provides fewer directives. Asked to explain this approach in more depth, he said that, unlike his "old school" colleagues in the company, he understood the importance of motivating and developing people and knew how to build on their strengths and lead them without directing them. He understood that it was better to be a coach and a mentor and to ask questions than to be directive or give people the answers to questions. He said he worked to guide people through a problem-solving process that was developmental in nature. This involved interacting with the store management team to facilitate self-discovery and change through thought provoking questioning. He provided both hypothetical and remembered examples and insisted that his approach was radically different from any of the other district managers he had worked with. He answered very specific questions in significant detail about how he coached his store managers, which we then captured in intricate detail in our notes. It sounded promising.

The next day, in the second step of our research process, we went into the field to observe him in action as he visited stores. As silent observers, we transcribe actual interactions between the field executive and the store manager. We meticulously capture the issues observed and discussed (or not discussed), any advice or directives that are provided and when the store manager makes notes of directions or directives given. We are especially sensitive to the instances of defensive reasoning and "fancy footwork" used by the store manager or others to avoid responsibility and embarrassment. The first store visit we observed in this case lasted slightly more than two hours, and we had numerous pages of notes documenting the District Manager's actual approach.

After leaving the store, we sat down with the DM to de-brief.

"Was this a typical visit?" he was asked. He replied that, yes, it was very typical.

"This is the way in which you visit stores, as you described in detail yesterday?"

"Yes," he said, "this visit was an example of what I was talking about."

"How many directives do you think you gave to the store manager over the course of our visit?"

"Probably just a few," he said, "maybe three or four. As I said, I keep my directives to an absolute minimum."

"So you would be surprised to learn that over the course of that two hour visit, you gave 67 directives, 32 of which the store manager made note of on his pad."

When we referred to the transcript and provided the DM with specific examples of his directives, he was shocked and resisted at first. He could not believe that, in practice, his leadership approach was identical the "old school" approach he criticized and was totally incongruent with the intended approach he had mapped out to us the day before. In spite of his apparently sincere and well-intentioned efforts to change and re-package his style, his fundamental approach was no different from that of his colleagues in other organizations.

Our observations went far beyond the number of directives given and recorded. We also noted that this DM failed to manage his ignorance and that his leadership focus was misplaced.

What did he need to know that he didn't know regarding the veracity of the store manager's accounting of performance and assertions of ability and commitment to change? What did the DM leave the store assuming -

not knowing - about the condition of the store team and the store manager's ability to develop his team? What did the DM assume about what the store manager learned about himself, his team and the root causes of the problems identified and addressed? Moreover, what was learned about why the 67 variances were not seen and addressed or why many of them had recurred? Or about why the store manager took down only 32 directives and which directives he noted and omitted, and why? We addressed all of these questions and more with the DM.

"What value did you add today?" we asked.

"I think the store manager got a lot out of the visit," he replied.

"Like what?"

"Well, I think for one thing he learned that store recovery wasn't happening and that he needed to work with his team to make sure the store is fully recovered when the doors open each day."

"How do you know for a fact that he learned this and that he knows how to "work" with his team to make sure the store is consistently and effectively recovered each day?"

"I guess I don't."

"Would that be important for you to know?"

"Yes, of course."

"How could you find out?"

"I could ask and test it out."

"OK, so then you don't know for a fact what, if anything, the store manager got out of your visit today, is that fair?"

"Yes. Actually I've been assuming in all my store visits that I've been making a difference when it's possible I haven't."

"What leads you to that conclusion?"

"Well, for one thing, if the store managers were really learning, I wouldn't be seeing and correcting the same problems in the same stores over and over again."

"What does that tell you?"

"Maybe the store manager in this case doesn't know how to develop his team."

"What else?"

"Maybe his team hasn't been trained in the core processes or doesn't know what's expected of it."

"If all this is true, what would it tell you about the store manager?"

"That he might not be willing or able to do the job."

"What else?"

"That he's either wrong for the job or needs development."

"So, who is responsible for building and upgrading the store management team in your district? In other words, who is responsible for ensuring that the right people are being hired, promoted, empowered, developed, retained or discharged as store managers in your district?"

"I am. But what's becoming clear to me is that the way I've been visiting stores has been doing the store manager's job for him. I've been focusing on the store and not the store manager and covering up for him and me... Geez, this is depressing. All this time I thought I was adding value and making a difference when I wasn't."

This initial realization proved to be a watershed experience for this DM. We'd like to say that this is an isolated case. Unfortunately, this DM is far from alone. He is like virtually every other retail field executive we have observed in action, in countless store visits across a broad spectrum of retail organizations. They all have a professed way of doing things and then they have the way in which they actually do them. Seldom are they the same.

## THEORIES OF ACTION

In Action Science, there are two classes of theories of action.

The professed way of doing things is called the *"Espoused Theory."* This is the approach you intend to use in order to achieve an objective or resolve a problem. We call this your *Intended Approach*. In the case of our DM, this was how he intended to visit stores in his district: to ask questions of them and listen, then coach, rather than provide answers, direction or directives.

The *"Theory in Use"* is a term used for the approach you actually use to achieve an outcome or resolve a problem. In spite of what you may *intend* to do, this is what you *actually* do. We refer to this as your *Actual Approach*. In the case of our DM, this amounted to the manipulative way he controlled the store manager and store environment through directives disguised as (leading) questions.

There may or may not be any overlap between a person's Intended Approach, or what they or profess to do, and their Actual Approach, that which they actually do. Typically, people are not even aware of the mismatch that exists between their intentions and their actions.

## THE PREVAILING APPROACH TO RETAIL MANAGEMENT

Our years of field research in the retail sector have produced overwhelming evidence that there is a common approach that retail field executives use in visiting stores to improve store performance. This actual approach, as well as its accompanying problem-solving routines, consistently produces a variety of undesirable and unintended results. Yet, executives continue with the approach, blind to the fact that it is not working. Thus, they become highly skilled at doing something that is either marginally productive at best or counterproductive at worst. This can be referred to as our "skilled incompetence." It is what we do very well that either achieves unwanted results or does not achieve desired results. Those undesirable results are, essentially, putting the field executive in the position of repeatedly addressing the same problem stores with the same failed approach, resulting in even more store problems. That is the picture of an executive who has become skilled at his incompetence, caught in a recurring loop of dysfunctional leadership.

So what is this prevailing, actual approach to retail field management? Our research points to this:

*If you want to improve store conditions, team performance and results, you must:*

➢  *Tell store managers what you expect.*

➢  *Inspect what you expect.*

➢  *Point out deviations.*

➢  *Provide direction (in the form of suggestions, advice, leading questions or directives) to correct the deviations.*

➢  *Follow up on performance to make sure it gets done.*

In short, we refer to this as the *Inspect/Direct/Correct* (IDC) approach to retail field management. As a theory of action, this approach, and the various store visit routines derived from it, is seriously flawed for two reasons. First, it is based on a variety of unsubstantiated beliefs and assumptions that are justified by various forms of defensive reasoning.

Consider the following questions asked by field coaches of field executives during the assessment phase of development:

Regarding the actions of *telling* and *inspecting*:

-   *What factual assurance would you have that simply telling a
    direct report what is expected would result in consistently effective
    action, or even action at all? Have you told them before what you
    told them today? (In almost all cases the answer is "yes.") Then
    why did you need to tell them again?*

-   *Why would continual and frequent supervisor-driven inspections
    be necessary if the communication of expectations had been
    understood?*

-   *What would such inspecting assure, and why? What objective
    data confirms such assurance beyond subjective experience?*

-   *What do these actions of telling and inspecting assume regarding
    how people learn and why such deviations occurred in the first
    place, or why they recur? What is the supporting data that would
    confirm such assumptions?*

-   *What does the necessity of such inspections assume about the
    actual competence and commitment of the store manager? What
    objective data has been produced to either confirm or refute such
    assumptions?*

-   *What would happen if supervisor-driven inspections were not
    made? Why? What evidence supports such conclusions?*

-   *How might a decline in store performance in the absence of, or as
    a result of, such inspections be otherwise accounted for? On what
    factual basis besides your opinion?*

-   *What assumptions would deter the field executive from openly
    testing the hypothesis that supervisor-driven inspections create
    their own necessity? How could this hypothesis be tested?*

-   *Finally, given that periodic inspections and evaluations are
    necessary as a means of determining progress, assessing
    performance or identifying opportunities for development or
    needs for change (not all inspections and evaluations are created*

> *equal!), how might such inspections be built into the basic stewardship and accountability structure of the store manager position? Specifically, how might necessary, periodic and objective inspections and evaluations be initiated, arranged and executed by the store manager? This might occur, for example, through improved, developmentally designed and tested internal store inspection routines performed regularly by the store manager and store management team, as well as through store manager-planned and solicited external store inspections by the VP, DM, other store managers (peers), or even other qualified members of the district or regional store support staff.*

Next, regarding the actions of *pointing out* deviations and providing some form of *direction* to *correct* the deviations:

- *What would happen if the field executive didn't point out any deviations or provide any direction to the store manager in order to fix the store? What's the reliable evidence to support such a conclusion?*

- *How might a decline in store performance in the absence of such pointing and directing be otherwise accounted for? What factual basis besides your opinion do you have to support this?*

- *What assumptions might deter a field executive from openly testing the hypothesis that his pointing and directing was contributing to performance blindness and dependency in the store manager? How could this hypothesis be tested?*

Finally, regarding the efficacy of the overall approach itself:

- *What objective, empirical evidence supports the hypotheses that make this IDC approach necessary and effective?*

- *What's the actual, verifiable ratio of hits to misses in terms of predicted outcomes using this IDC approach in visiting stores?*

In putting these and other related questions to numerous field executives (i.e. Regional or Territory Vice Presidents and District Managers) over the years, it became evident to them and to us that the *inspecting, directing and correcting* approach is based on the unfounded and, in fact, erroneous beliefs that:

- *Telling store managers what you expect will result in the performance of those expectations.*

- *People learn by being repeatedly told what to do and how to do it.*

- *People do what they're told to do the way you expect them to do it, and*

- *If you didn't inspect what you expected, the store manager would either not do it, or not do it right.*

These beliefs are, in turn, based on the following unsubstantiated assumptions:

- *The reason the store managers don't/won't do what they're supposed to do, or do it wrong is because they are not sufficiently competent, engaged or committed.*

- *Because the store managers are not sufficiently competent, engaged and committed, they need constant and frequent supervision to help them see what they can't see and do what they can't or aren't doing, and*

- *If we (i.e. field executives) didn't inspect, point out and direct store managers to correct deviations in store conditions, stores would get progressively worse.*

Finally, continued use of this prevailing IDC approach, as well as the beliefs and assumptions themselves, are justified through the defensive reasoning alluded to above. Such reasoning, in this case, takes the form of certain well-known thinking fallacies. Specifically, we find that many, if not most, field executives initially argue in favor this approach because:

- *They wrongly reason that their use of the approach justifies their using the approach: "We're using this approach because we lack confidence in the store manager's competence and commitment and we know the store manager is not sufficiently competent or committed because we are using this approach" (circular argument).*

- *They assert that they "know" store managers are insufficiently competent and committed on the sole basis of what they've learned or concluded from their own subjective experience: "I know these store managers are insufficiently competent and committed because I work with them and know them" (self-referential argument).*

- *They insist these conclusions are confirmed whenever the field executive doesn't visit the store for several weeks and the store managers don't or won't take the initiative to maintain or improve store conditions, while failing to acknowledge the possibility that these store managers aren't performing in part because of the way they've been managed over the years (self-fulfilling argument).*

- *They argue that they use this approach because that's they way they've been taught and that's what's expected of them (self-excusing argument).*

- *They argue that the way they're visiting stores and interacting with store managers is producing good enough results, confusing weak correlation with causation (post-hoc argument).*

- *They assume that their boss would disapprove of their visiting stores differently and refuse, out of fear, to test such an assumption by discussing their concern directly with their boss (self-sealing argument).*

The second reason this prevailing IDC approach is flawed has to do with its observed and reported results, both in terms of the failure of consistently achieving targeted results and in the production of a variety of harmful and undesirable results. To better appreciate how these undesirable results are produced, it might be helpful to elaborate further on how the IDC approach illustrated in Figure 1 below might play out in a typical store visit.

# FIGURE 1:
## THE INSPECT/DIRECT/CORRECT APPROACH (IDC)

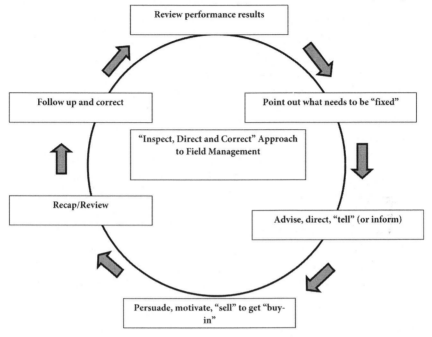

Utilizing this approach, the retail field executive (usually a VP or DM) will enter the store (announced or unannounced), check out the front end and walk around until he hooks up with the store manager. He will then engage the store manager in a general conversation about the overall condition of the store. After greetings and small talk, the inspection will begin in earnest. The field executive will walk the store with the store manager and possibly the assistant manager or various department managers to inspect store conditions. Perhaps he'll do a perimeter visit, where he starts at the front end of the store, then walks around the store, followed by a classic four-by-four inspection walk down each aisle. Afterward, those involved might move into the backroom, then possibly the restrooms and lunch room. The participants would then end up either at the front or back of the store, or in the store manager's office, to recap the visit. This is a typical routine, although there are variations of this pattern. Most experienced DMs and VPs have developed their own routines for visiting stores, but the underlying approach itself, and the defensive orientation that drives it, are always the same.

In this process, the field executive is looking for shelves full of product, correct pricing, correct signage, clean, uncluttered aisles, end caps and displays that are placed in accordance with merchandising plan-o-grams, and active customer service and up-selling on the sales floor.

The executive is also looking to ensure that the look and feel of the store is consistent with the brand promise, that safety, quality and merchandizing standards are followed, that programs dictated by store support functions are being executed, and that associates on the floor are attending to customer needs. Essentially, the executive is walking through the store to inspect and make certain that store conditions meet company standards.

As the entourage works its way through the store, department by department, deviations will be pointed out, and there will be some discussion about what needs to be done. There are various ways a field executive will approach this. Some might be direct, saying: "Why isn't this shelf filled?" or "This display isn't consistent with the plan" or "These prices don't reflect our current sale" or "This signage is not current."

Our DM who liked to challenge his store managers with his more modern leadership methodology used a tactic that was more of an indirect control-based approach. He would walk up to an aisle with empty space on the shelf and say, "Tell me what you see here."

This, in theory, requires that the store manager identify the problem *himself*, tell the DM what is going to be done about it, and then add it to the checklist. In reality, however, this tactic employs the guess-what-I'm-seeing-and-thinking game, which plays right in to the DM's need to control the situation and the store manager. If the store manager doesn't see what the DM is seeing, however, more leading questions are used to direct the store manager to the departure from standards. For example, "Is this price consistent with today's ad?" or "Is this display where it needs to be?" Then, if the store manager doesn't produce the solution that the DM believes is appropriate, the DM again resorts to leading questions to direct the store manager to the DM's solution, e.g. "Don't you think this display would result in more sales if it were placed here instead of there?"

Bottom line to this approach: it is still the DM who has to control the situation by bringing attention to the problem and providing the best solution, even if doing so is masked by leading questions.

Once the deviation has been pointed out, the conversation typically moves to advising the store manager on what needs to be done to rectify the problem. Usually the problem is so minor that pointing it out seems to be all that's needed to fix it. But this conclusion has often proven erroneous. The obvious and simple departures from standards become more complicated issues when we find that these same variances have been pointed out before, and not just once before, but more than once or twice. And not to someone new, but to the same experienced store team who, by all accounts, should have spotted and corrected such deviations without being told. Or, better yet, who should have prevented such a variance to begin with. Simple problems are often deceptively complex.

We have observed that in most cases the feedback by the field executives consists of: (1) general, often meaningless evaluations (e.g. "Your store doesn't look crisp," or "Your store conditions are poor"); (2) unsubstantiated, experienced-based attributions, or causal explanations (e.g. "This empty shelf tells me that your logistics manager isn't shooting the holes in these aisles"); (3) broad-brush, or vague, direction or advice (e.g. "You need to get on your people and make sure they're on board with this program and know how to execute it"); and (4) ambiguous, mixed messages (e.g. "This is your store, and you need to take the initiative and do whatever it takes to make plan" followed by "Just make sure you don't do anything stupid and check with me in these areas before you take action").

These four errors have one critical characteristic in common, besides being controlling and directive in nature. They are all unactionable. Because they are so general and inconsistent, they can only serve to confuse and frustrate managers and associates, undermining accountability as they attempt to guess what, specifically, they are supposed to do. They assume they understand what their boss wants and attempt to do what they're told, all the while privately, if not publicly, abdicating responsibility for the outcomes of their actions.

Meanwhile, the problems continue to proliferate and recur, not only because of the four errors enumerated above, but because the problems addressed are the wrong problems, a subject we will deal with in great depth in the next chapter.

So, the field executive has done what? Inspected conditions, pointed out deviations and provided (yet again) more mixed and/or meaningless instructions to correct them. There may have been some level of persuasion involved to sell the idea to the store manager on the importance of making the changes, but the unspoken, message seems clear: "Get it fixed now, and do it my way."

Throughout this process, the store manager, assistant manager and department managers have been dutifully making checklists of all the items requiring attention. At the end of the visit, the executive meets briefly with the store manager and the team and "recaps" the visit. This recap usually consists of the VP and/or DM evaluating the store and the store team, sending the mixed message that they are doing a good job but need to do better (interpreted as "You're not doing a good job"), attributing their successes and failures ("opportunities") to unsubstantiated causes and going through the list of deviations and correctives. Agreement by all is solicited and, of course, given by all enthusiastically and without hesitation or reservation.

Finally, the visiting executive usually requests that an action plan with projected completion dates be put together by the store manager and emailed to him. It is understood that the purpose of such an assignment is to hold the store manager accountable for doing what's on the list. The tacit assumption of the field executive is likewise transparent. Unless this assignment is made and complied with, the corrections likely won't be made. (It is worth noting that such action plans have usually been requested of the same store manager regarding essentially the same issues on past occasions and were completed and submitted by the store manager and accepted by the VP or DM without critical and collaborative review.)

At this point, the field executive will almost always say something like, "Now, before I leave, is there anything I can do to help *you*?"

Between the lines of the official response ("I can't think of anything right at the moment, but if I do, I'll be sure to call you") is the manager's undisclosed mental thought ("Please just leave my store as quickly as you can so that I can get back to work").

We should emphasize at this point that there are variations in store visit routines among different field executives. The scenario presented above to illustrate the IDC approach is a composite constructed from over a thousand observed actual store visits in a variety of chain retail organizations.

We're not insisting that all VPs and DMs visit their stores in exactly the same way. Rather, our contention is that the underlying approach to retail field management is virtually identical in every major retail organization we have researched and worked with to date, and we have no reason to suppose that there are significant exceptions.

This does not mean that there *are* no individual exceptions. It means that we have yet to observe one. In saying this, however, we must also be quick to caution any field executive reading this chapter not to assume that his approach is different. In too many instances where that assertion was made - as with the DM we described earlier - the actual approach turned out to be identical to the IDC approach. It is therefore very unlikely that your approach will be different.

After such store visits with VPs and DMs, we frequently ask, "Of the list of problems you pointed out in this store today, how many have you addressed before with this same store manager?"

Invariably, the response is, "Many (or most) of them."

Then the question is, "How many of the items that you pointed out and gave direction on today do you think a qualified store manager should be able to identify and solve on his own?"

Invariably, the response is, "All of them."

These field executives, who have pointed out the very same problems to the same store managers multiple times, believe the store managers should not need this level of direction, yet they keep providing it, in spite of the undesirable results it generates.

## UNDESIRABLE RESULTS

Let's look more closely at the undesirable results, which have been repeatedly confirmed, not only by our own action research in the field, but by senior field executives in numerous major retail organizations. As you read through these results, reflect on your own experience and ask yourself if the stores within your stewardship struggle with any of the following challenges.

## INCONSISTENT RESULTS

Store results are inconsistent, either overall or in one or more key result areas of the store. One month the results are up, the next month they are down. In spite of what appear to be management's best efforts, the stores are not able to generate consistent results at-or-above plan in every sales, operational, service, and expense category. In some cases, stores that have been performing well for a period of time unexpectedly slip and become inconsistent in one or more result area and for reasons outside the store manager's awareness or control.

## ERRATIC EXECUTION

Some programs get executed well. Some do not. Yet the good and bad executions are often by the same team in the same store with no identifiable reason for the discrepancy. Problems occur. In response, management addresses them, gets comfortable that the problems are resolved, and then moves on to something else, believing they have fixed the problems. Then, some time later, the same or similar performance problems recur. Management addresses them again, focusing again on quick-fix solutions to get them solved, gets comfortable that the problems are solved and then moves on to something else, believing they have fixed the problems. Then, some time later, the same or similar problems recur. You see where this is going.

What makes this phenomenon so complex and its solution so elusive is the fact that core, systemic performance problems present themselves in a variety of seemingly unrelated ways. As a result, they defy simple solutions or simplistic approaches to change. An Asian proverb suggests that for every complex problem there are 10,000 simple, *in*correct solutions. Recurring problems are usually complex performance problems. When such problems are addressed at the wrong level in the wrong way, the result is erratic execution.

## UNDERMINING OF ACCOUNTABILITY

Field executives often suggest that they are "holding their managers accountable" for performance, and store managers often say, with great conviction, "I *own* my store." Both assertions give cause for doubt. If field executives' efforts at "holding" store managers accountable were really resulting in store managers truly owning their own stores, how do we explain the fact that when confronted by deviations and sub-standard performance, many store managers engage in defensive reasoning and fancy footwork, offering unsubstantiated reasons for non-performance and shifting blame, pointing fingers, explaining away variances, defending team members, justifying actions taken or not taken, or minimizing the problems?

Another common response is for a store manager to explain why the problems were missed and what's being done to fix them or that they are known problems and remedies are already in process. If that is true, why haven't they been fixed? Why do they recur? Why must the field executive draw attention to them? If the store manager really *owned* the store, would we even see these problems to the degree we do?

Field leaders continually seem to be seduced by these excuses, buying into defensive reasoning that is designed to justify actions taken or shift the blame to get the store manager off the hook. The field executives themselves undermine accountability when they take control of the store, pointing out deviations and providing direction to correct them. They assume ownership of the problem when they produce a solution. Then, when the solution doesn't work, it was the field leader's solution, not the store manager's. There is little to no accountability in this structure.

By reducing the store manager to a note taker in store visits and making the field executive a compliance auditor, the directives given by the DM or VP do not result in correcting the problem. When that becomes evident by a recurrence of the problem, the store manager can simply say, "I did what you told me to do." The store manager has thereby abdicated his responsibilities to his boss, who gladly assumed them for reasons we will discuss later. In this process, which no doubt occurs every single day in every field leader's region of the country, those leaders are undermining, through their own actions, the very accountability they say they so desperately want to create.

## CREATING AN ANTI-LEARNING ENVIRONMENT

Store managers, too, often don't anticipate store problems or think for themselves beyond established or required protocol. Why should they when their bosses are either doing the thinking for them or dictating what needs to be done? In many cases, critical thinking and true learning have essentially come to a halt. All they have to do is follow the program and implement prescribed "best practices." The role of the store manager has been reduced to that of a custodian or operator. In an attempt to fix a problem, he often acts by rote, out of his experience, instead of reflectively. Store managers are not being developed and encouraged to anticipate or think through the complex performance problems they face, or the likely success of the solutions they take. By taking control of the store manager's environment, the field executive and store support directors effectively release that manager of the responsibility to learn and grow. This, in turn, creates what we call an anti-learning environment. The stores are not "learning stores." The districts are not "learning districts." All the while, the field executive wonders why store managers are not learning from their mistakes, why they fail to anticipate and effectively resolve performance problems, and why they aren't getting expected results.

## MAKING MANAGEMENT THE PRIMARY CUSTOMER

When we coach, we're always curious to see where store management is focused. Unfortunately, in most cases, the real customer is not the person who has walked through the door to buy something; it is the store manager's boss. In most retail organizations the store manager will attend to the DM's or VP's needs, requests and directives with top priority, often at the expense of the customer. The store manager and other members of the store team are so busy fixing the store to please their boss(es) or cover up problems that there's little-to-no time to serve the customers. There are too many programs, initiatives and standards to comply with, too many controls to work around and too many bosses to please.

Case in point: I was recently shopping at one of our clients' stores, searching for an item that I couldn't find. After wandering around in vain for several minutes, I came across the store manager, who was busily giving directions to other associates while working to set up an end-cap display. At the appropriate moment I asked, "Can you please tell me where to find appliance light bulbs?" The store manager replied, "I'm not sure exactly, but it is down this center aisle about 9 or 10 rows and then down to the left." With that he resumed his task.

What did his action reveal as this store manager's priority - the customer or the task? And why would the task be his priority? Before leaving, the answer became apparent as the store manager was seen walking through the store with the RVP and DM. Who, then, was the store manager's primary customer? The paying customer, the one we say we are the most focused on serving, certainly wasn't. This experience provides one of countless examples we have encountered as customers and researchers, even in companies touted for their excellence in customer service.

## STRIVING FOR COMPLIANCE AT THE EXPENSE OF COMMITMENT

The name of the game for a store manager is to figure out what his boss wants and then to give it to him. *He's the customer.* Store managers have learned to comply with what they've been told to do. This, of course, compromises engagement and internal commitment to excellence. The IDC approach assumes that positive and energized store managers and associates are fully engaged and likewise committed to the solutions that the DM provides to their problems. Unfortunately, compliance is not the same as commitment. Human beings have little commitment to ideas that they're directed to adopt. As we will discuss in more detail later, commitment comes from participating in the creation of solutions that work. We are rarely committed to directives that are merely handed down to us; more likely, we are merely compliant.

## ATTITUDES TOWARD A VISION: FROM APATHY TO COMPLIANCE TO COMMITMENT

All executives say they want employees to be "committed" to the organization and its vision and values. But what does commitment really mean? What does it look like? How does a "committed" employee actually behave?

In his book *The Fifth Discipline (1990, Currency-Doubleday, pp. 218-220)*, Peter Senge makes the case that true commitment is rare in today's organizations. He submits that most of the time, what passes for commitment is actually compliance. What is the difference? Senge's brief descriptions below help explain the varying attitudes, ranging from apathy at one extreme, to commitment at the other.

## POSSIBLE ATTITUDES TOWARD A VISION

*Commitment: The person wants the vision and will make it happen, creating whatever "laws" (structures, processes or policies) are needed to do so. This person not only exhibits a high level of energy and initiative, but a high tolerance for uncertainty and willingness to risk and sacrifice.*

*Enrollment: This person wants the vision and will do whatever can be done within the "spirit of the law" to make it happen. This attitude is characterized by high energy, moderate sacrifice, and low risk and tolerance to uncertainty.*

*Genuine compliance: This person sees the benefits of the vision and does everything expected and more, following the letter of the law. "Good soldier."*

*Formal compliance: On the whole, this person sees the benefits of the vision, does what's expected and no more. "Pretty good soldier."*

*Grudging compliance: This person does not see the benefits of the vision, but also does not want to lose his job. He does enough of what's expected because he has to, but also lets it be known that he is not really on board.*

> **Noncompliance:** *This person does not see the benefits of the vision and will not do what's expected. "I won't do it; you can't make me."*

> **Apathy:** *This person is neither for nor against the vision. No interest. No energy. "Is it five o'clock yet?"*

In most organizations, employees hover between *formal compliance* and *genuine compliance.* How about in the retail sector? Is there even an appetite for the truly committed employee – an employee who creates whatever rules, policies, processes or structures are necessary to perform at a level consistent with the organization's vision and values?

Let's explore the difference between compliance and commitment by looking at two contrasting real life examples taken from the hospitality sector:

The motto of one of the world's renowned luxury hotel chains is "We are ladies and gentlemen serving ladies and gentlemen." This vision seems to be evidenced by the legendary service these hotels consistently offer their guests.

This was put to the test one evening several years ago when I was staying in one of their hotels. Very late at night, a McDonald's commercial appeared on television, featuring a "Big Mac" value meal. It was around 10 p.m. My body responded with an instant craving. I had to have a Big Mac. I resisted by insisting to myself that it was late and I didn't want to go out looking for a McDonald's restaurant.

Then it hit me. I was staying at an award-winning hotel, known for its unsurpassed service. Others who had stayed there had told stories of remarkable instances of guest service where hotel staff members, regardless of their role, would solve problems or run errands for guests far beyond the call of duty. I decided to put the hotel's service reputation to the test. I called the bell desk and the bellman greeted me by name and asked how he could be of service. I told him my story and then asked if he would go to McDonald's for me.

There was a brief pause on the other end of the phone and then this young bellman said, "Sir, I've never been asked to do this before, but I would be delighted to go to McDonald's for you." I gave him my order and twenty minutes later he arrived at my door with my Big Mac Value Meal. I opened the door and he greeted me, smiled, handed me my meal and said, "Enjoy." He left without even waiting for me to pay him. I was amazed.

Later, I wrote the hotel manager a letter of commendation for the exceptional service at his hotel and noted the bellman by name and the example of his commitment to their vision. I received a response from the manager, thanking me for my letter and informing me that the bellman would be duly recognized and rewarded and then assuring me that had I asked anyone at the hotel to do the same thing, I would have enjoyed the same response.

Where was the bellman on the continuum of possible attitudes toward a vision? Clearly there was no policy or procedure for responding to a guest who suffered from a Big Mac attack. Apparently, this young man covered his post so that other guests would not be compromised and, with his own car, went to the nearby McDonald's and used his own money to buy me my meal. Who gave him approval to do so? No one. What authorized him to do this? The vision, with its motto, "We are ladies and gentlemen serving ladies and gentlemen," is what authorized him. This young bellman made it happen by *creating* policy and procedure. He was clearly committed. In my experience, this quality of service is not the exception in this hotel chain, but the rule.

Now for the contrasting example: On another occasion I stayed at a different hotel, which was equally expensive and which also had a mission promising exceptional service. I arrived late at night and slept in the next morning. It was 11:15 and I decided to order some breakfast. I called room service and was greeted by name by a pleasant woman who asked for my order. I said that I would like to order some breakfast. She replied, again very politely, "I'm sorry sir, breakfast ended at 11:00, but I'd be delighted to serve you some lunch." I told her that I had just awakened and that I truly wanted breakfast. She politely held her ground that breakfast hours were over. I again decided to test the hotels' *commitment* to service:

> *"I really don't want lunch, I want breakfast. What can you work out for me?"*

> *"I'm sorry sir, I would love to serve you breakfast, but I can't. The cooks have changed the kitchen over for lunch."*

> *"So there is nothing you can do?"*

> *"No sir, I'm sorry."* With this response, I decided to push the *"service"* envelope even further.

> *"Well, do you have a club sandwich?"*

*"Yes, we do."*

*"If I ordered a club sandwich, would you be able to put the toasted bread and bacon on a separate dish?"*

*(Pause) "Yes, I can do that."*

*"OK, good. Do you have a fruit plate with yogurt?"*

*"Yes, we do."*

*"Great, can I get some orange juice also?"*

*"Yes, of course."*

*"And coffee?"*

*"Not a problem."*

*"Let's see then. If I understand correctly, I can have toast, bacon, fruit and yogurt, orange juice and coffee – is that right?"*

*(Chuckling) "Yes, that's right. We can serve you all that."*

*"You see, I can have breakfast."*

*"Yes you can."*

As pleasant as this young lady was, she was not committed to the hotel's mission of exceptional service. She was genuinely compliant, a "good soldier," bound by the "letter of the law." Even if I had wanted pancakes and eggs, a commitment to service would have found a way to provide them. This person would have found a way to make it happen if she was truly committed to their vision.

In the retail sector, field executives don't manage their organizations in such a way that fosters *commitment*. At best, they are looking for "good soldiers" who exhibit *genuine compliance*, in the name of consistency.

## FOSTERING ASSOCIATE DEPENDENCY

Store managers and associates who have become dependent upon their field leaders to solve complex problems or "work the hierarchy" for them are not taking responsibility for their stores. They're relying upon their managers to think for them. They've been trained to expect that. Too many store managers today are functioning more as operators than general managers and leaders. Our research is very clear on this point: The IDC approach that field executives are using as they work with store managers often creates an unhealthy dependency on both leaders and experience. This dependency is extraordinarily widespread. Store managers functioning as operators, running their stores by the book, can't seem to come up with novel ideas or approaches to improving performance or anticipating and solving complex problems. Even if they are experienced and have a stable team that executes well, they are often not able to think beyond traditional routines or what they've been told. They have become over-reliant on their bosses' experience to identify opportunities and come up with solutions.

This dependency gets replicated throughout the store. Assistant managers and department managers are dependent upon the store manager to tell them what to do, how to do it and when to get it done. Following is a painful case study of a large organization that came face-to-face with the dependency it had fostered.

## HOW A RESTRUCTURING BROUGHT AN ORGANIZATION TO ITS KNEES

A large retail company was trying to fix a grossly under-performing division in a large region, deemed strategically significant to the company. In the process, the company was also testing a potential new management structure that the senior leaders believed would streamline operations and reduce significant cost from the business.

The existing structure was fairly classic. Here was the hierarchy:

➢ *Regional Vice President*

➢ *District Manager*

➢ *Store Manager*

➢ *Assistant Store Manager*

➤ *Department Managers*

The new structure eliminated the District Managers and put the RVPs in a direct supervisory role over the Store Managers. The Store Managers were turned into Group Store Managers, who oversaw multiple stores, not just a single one. The new hierarchy looked like this:

➤ *Regional Vice President*

➤ *Group Store Manager (over multiple stores)*

➤ *Assistant Store Manager*

➤ *Department Manager*

This was a large division, so the elimination of district managers and the creation of Group Store Managers offered significant cost savings.

A new division president started the process by interviewing all the existing RVPs and DMs for the new RVP positions. A few were selected from the current team but most were brought into the division from other areas of the company, and the new RVP team was established.

The new RVPs immediately went to work interviewing previous DMs and store managers for the new Group Store Manager positions. In the majority of cases, the RVPs did not have any experience with the managers they were evaluating. They did their best under a very short timeline, in many cases drawing from a single meeting to select the managers they felt could step up to the new level of Group Store Manager.

They implemented the structure. Coinciding with the implementation was an aggressive action learning intervention intended to develop the leadership capability of the division's senior executives and RVPs. And, in an effort to reduce overhead expense, a large percentage of the store employees were reduced from full-time (many working significant overtime) to part-time status, significantly reducing their incomes and putting their health insurance at risk. This resulted in substantial turnover and plummeting employee morale. All of this was happening at the same time.

This division was completely typical of the retail organizations we have been describing: inconsistent performance, erratic execution, extremely low levels of personal accountability, little customer focus, and highly compliant employees who were dependent upon their bosses for virtually all direction.

The extraordinarily high level of dependency caught the division leaders by surprise and led to near disaster. As they implemented the structure, they removed DMs with responsibility over 10 to 15 stores and gave RVPs, most of whom were new to their areas, direct oversight responsibility for two or three times that number of stores. The store managers, who previously had the focus of a DM 15 to 25 percent of the time, suddenly had access to an RVP maybe 5 percent of the time, and those store managers now had responsibility for more than just one store. Assistant store managers, who had been taking direction from a store manager the majority of the time, now only had access to that person half of the time. Because of the high turnover rate in the employee ranks, in many cases the assistant store managers had open positions or new employees who were not trained to do their jobs. Because of conflicting needs and simple scheduling limitations, there were many times in prime selling hours of the day when neither a manager nor an assistant manager was present in the store.

Store operations derailed. Store personnel, who were accustomed to taking direction from one of the managers, suddenly had no one providing it. Many of the employees responsible for day-to-day operations had quit. The number of out of stock items skyrocketed. Storage rooms filled up with inventory, as no one was providing direction on what to do with it all. With no one overseeing store conditions, they became a mess. Compliance with merchandising plan-o-grams faltered. Strategic national promotions were often not effectively executed. Sales got worse.

Why did all of this happen? Clearly, the division took on too much radical change at one time, but why couldn't the workers in the stores step up, as management expected, and do the jobs they had been doing before?

The answer, in retrospect, was quite obvious: for generations, this organization's leaders had fostered extreme dependency in the way they led the organization. Store managers took too much direction from their DMs. They apparently weren't capable of functioning without that direction, let alone while trying to take on the management of another store. Within the store ranks, people did what they were told. The manager or assistant manager provided daily, hour-by-hour direction to line employees. Without it, nothing got done. Employees did not know how to react. They had never been expected to think on their own or show initiative. Directive-by-directive, day-by-day, they had been turned into "good soldiers" who did what they were told and rarely asked questions. With no one around to provide the direction or pose questions to, they did the best they could, which wasn't even close to good enough. Management became very clear about the result of fostering a dependent environment.

All of the "undesirable results" addressed earlier in this chapter can easily be attributed to external factors and/or store manager incompetence, and too often are. This is an easy way out for field executives, particularly those who placed the store managers in position to begin with and are responsible for developing them. At some point the field executive needs to look in the mirror and question his own leadership approach and orientation to action.

Most of the field executives we work with admit that their approach to field leadership is fundamentally flawed. In light of the evidence, these executives know that the way they've been visiting stores isn't consistently producing the results they want, expect or might otherwise achieve.

With this admission comes the profound realization that the undesirable results are defensively motivated, as is the IDC approach itself. As we will learn in Chapter 4, one significant reason VPs and DMs persist in visiting stores with such a control-based approach is a deeply ingrained defensive orientation to action and leadership. Such an orientation, we will find, influences all of us in the tacit design of our actions, reactions and interactions. Simply stated, the defensive way field executives visit stores is perfectly designed to produce the undesirable results achieved. The supervisor-driven, control-based IDC approach isn't working.

## THE CURSE OF SISYPHUS

These undesirable results and outcomes bring to mind the mythological Greek character, Sisyphus. The King of Corinth, Sisyphus was condemned for all eternity to roll a huge boulder up a mountain, only to have it roll back down again every time he neared the summit. He was caught in a fruitless exercise that he could never master.

If we look at this myth as a metaphor for retail field management, the boulder represents store performance. Sisyphus is, of course, the store manager or Retail Field Executive who feels condemned to a life of futility, pushing the boulder up an endless hill toward the summit of greatness, only to suffer the frustration and exhaustion that comes as a result of inconsistent performance.

The Curse of Sisyphus is a curse that retail executives have in large measure placed on themselves by virtue of a faulty approach to management that produces these undesirable results. In effect, we curse ourselves through our own skilled incompetence.

## KEY INSIGHTS FROM CHAPTER 1:

➢ *The way VPs and DMs have been visiting stores and managing in the field is virtually universal and is not working.*

➢ *The prevailing Inspect/Direct/Correct approach to field management generates inconsistent performance and results in erratic execution, an undermining of accountability, the creation of an anti-learning environment, and a dependent workforce in which associates make management the primary customer and are rewarded for being genuinely compliant, rather than committed.*

# CHAPTER 2

# SOLVING THE *WRONG* PROBLEMS AT BREAK-NECK SPEED

---

*In this chapter:*

➤ *Why is it necessary to repeatedly address the same problems in the same stores with the same store managers and associates?*

➤ *Why are multiple layers of management necessary to improve store conditions and performance?*

➤ *Why does speeding up change in stores so often result in stalled performance?*

---

Why do the same retail executives and managers have to deal with the same operational problems over and over again, day after day, month after month, year after year?

Because, our research concludes, field executives as well as store managers are focusing on the *wrong* problems.

This phenomenon of focusing on the wrong problems is, of course, related to the defensive, control-based IDC approach to field leadership. It is also exacerbated by the prevailing emphasis in retail today on the importance of *speed*. You know the mindset; the chances are pretty good that you even subscribe to it yourself: "We have to respond quickly to fix what is broken in the stores, and get the associates to respond quickly to comply with directives and company initiatives."

Put these two realities together and you will find most retail executives today *solving the wrong problems at break-neck speed.*

Later, we will address the paradox of speed that compromises performance, but first let's explore how the majority of retail executives have become so proficient at solving the wrong problems.

We have found that all store problems fall into one or more of four categories with one common root to all. This diagram, The Anatomy of a Problem, illustrates them:

# FIGURE 2:
## ANATOMY OF A PROBLEM

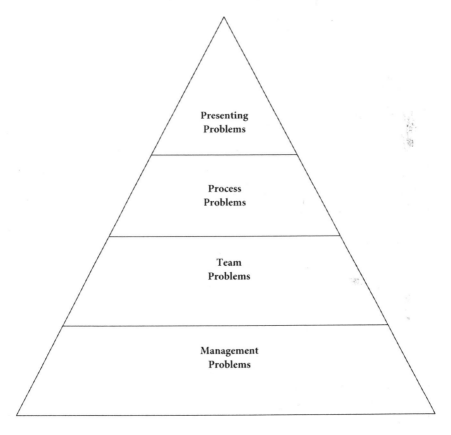

## PRESENTING PROBLEMS

The first layer of this problem pyramid is the *presenting problem*. *Presenting problems* include deviations from and lack of compliance with brand standards, expected store conditions, company standards or program requirements. Such a problem could be the difference between budgeted sales and actual sales; budgeted expenses and actual expenses; what is on the shelf versus what should be; what's on the merchandizing plan versus how the store is actually set up. It could be a physical variance in store conditions or a numerical variance in the operating numbers of the store.

The *presenting problem* is the problem at its most obvious level. It's the long checkout lines, the missing or misplaced product on the shelves, the incorrect pricing, the missing or out-of-date signage, the cluttered aisles, the dirty floors, the absence of service, the failure to up-sell, the excessive product loss, the disorganized backroom, and a variety of other deviations or variances too numerous to list. Typically, these are problems the store manager and store team are able to identify, and know how to prevent and fix, but frequently don't, or miss, leaving them to the RVP or DM to point out, which they habitually and willingly do on a recurring basis.

The experienced retail field executive can look at a situation and instantaneously identify what is wrong. When doing so, that executive is identifying a *presenting problem*. Unfortunately, as we are about to see, most executives stop right there and focus on fixing that *presenting problem*, as though it is *the* problem. The *presenting problem* is where the majority of field executives spend the majority of their time. However, the problem's simplicity is often deceiving, particularly when the variance is recurring.

When *presenting problems* are simple, routine and non-recurring, and when they can be quickly corrected, they are what we term *low-leverage problems*. When they are non-routine and recurring in nature, they are more complex and become *high-leverage execution problems*. Resolving these requires more time and a different approach.

## PROCESS PROBLEMS

The second layer problem is a *process problem*. Processes support and roll up into larger, strategic approaches and include various routines and operating procedures for decision-making, program execution, problem-solving and quality assurance and improvement. *Process problems* are often a contributing cause of certain *presenting problems*. They include not only the utilization of incorrect processes, but also the incorrect utilization or non-utilization of established processes. They also include the lack of process alignment with larger strategic or operational initiatives and/or a breakdown in process design, effectiveness or support. At this level, there is a fundamental breakdown in process that is contributing to the *presenting problem*. To assess whether a *presenting problem* is rooted in process, one might ask:

> ➢ *What processes, or routines, are relevant to this presenting problem?*

➤ *Are the processes actually in place in the store?*

➤ *Are the people trained in the processes?*

➤ *Are the processes themselves effective or do they need to be modified to be effective?*

Questions that a store manager might ask himself to help him get to the heart of *process problems* could include:

➤ *Do the processes provide valid information that enables people to make effective decisions?*

➤ *Are they overly restrictive or burdensome in nature?*

➤ *Are they supportive of the company's strategies and programs?*

➤ *Are they aligned with the realities of the business?*

➤ *Are they aligned with established approaches, or espoused theories of action?*

➤ *Are they actually in place? Are people aware of them and trained to use them?*

These processes typically refer to:
o *Pre-designed and prescribed daily, weekly and monthly routines, including inspection, scheduling, recovery, set-up and other routines*

o *Policies and Procedures*

o *Operational Systems*

o *Customer Service Protocols*

If a store manager's answers to these questions are *yes*, then he should test to confirm that his assumptions are accurate and that, in fact, there are processes in place, that they are realistic and in alignment with the strategy and programs of the organization, and that the appropriate staff are aware of, trained on, and proficient in handling them.

If the answer to any of these questions is *no*, then the store manager needs to determine what is being done by those who own the various processes in the store to rectify the deficiencies.

If the store manager answers *yes* to all these questions, his answers are validated, and consistent results are *still* not being obtained, then process is *not* the problem. In such a case, the store manager is dealing with a deeper level problem, either a *team problem* or a *management problem*, both of which are complex and high-leverage execution problems.

Many managers are taught incorrectly that most problems are *process problems*. That is to say, if there is a problem in the store, more than likely there is a need for a process, or a modification to a process, to more clearly define exactly what is supposed to be done and how.

In the age of Total Quality Management, ISO certification, Six Sigma programs and the like, many organizations have committed extensive resources to create process solutions to performance challenges. Paradoxically, in certain cultures, the resulting processes and systems designed to minimize or eliminate error often create organizational defenses to avoid exposure and accountability. In many cases, the new processes designed by those who have been contaminated by the very culture they serve, are control-based. In other cases, the new systems and processes are so detailed that, rather than being "user friendly," they are cumbersome, complicated and confusing. We refer to this as the deadly 3Cs of process design.

This defensive orientation to process design, coupled with the 3Cs above, often results in widespread user resistance. Instead of a commitment to the execution of process requirements, there might be, at best, an attitude of "genuine compliance." What's more, faced with new, more sophisticated systems, users often create short cuts to simplify the prescribed process and avoid the exposure of incompetence. These simplified processes, or sub-routines, become defensive routines that undermine effectiveness. In such cases, the store manager may indeed have a complex, high-leverage *process problem*. Such a problem would involve a process that is too cumbersome, too complex *and* too confusing and therefore threatening the desired level of performance. All this would make it a *team problem* as well.

Another drawback of excessive process focus is its potential for turning associates into unthinking robots. On a manufacturing assembly line, strict adherence to process helps ensure consistency and product quality. In the retail environment, where the customer's buying experience and satisfaction is the driver of success and profitability, overemphasis on process can turn an organization into an army of numb, albeit "good soldiers," executing the latest programs, treating their superiors as their customers, complying with a myriad of processes and ignoring the needs of their *real* customers.

Finally, process design, regardless of its quality, is only as good as the results derived from sound and consistent execution. Processes are tools. People design processes and use them. Most of the time, *presenting problems* are caused more directly by defensive process design bias and execution problems nested in the team. To stop at the process level will usually result in recurring problems.

## TEAM PROBLEMS

An organization can have perfectly clear, well-defined, highly efficient processes, but without trained, capable, engaged and accountable people to implement them, nothing will happen.

If those perfectly clear, well-defined, highly efficient processes are being implemented by untrained or incapable people with uncommitted attitudes, then you most likely have a *team problem*. *Team problems* are execution problems and involve either a failure to perform or inconsistent, erratic performance. *Team problems* can stem from unfilled staffing needs, improper placement, team member resistance and/or deficits in team member experience, knowledge, skill or engagement.

Unfortunately, most *team problems* are not easy to define. More often than not, staffing, training, capability or skill deficiencies are not the real issues. The real problems stem from defensive action, the presence of competing commitments or the absence of internal commitment. These issues in turn stem from a lack of empowerment and learning. To ascertain whether a *presenting problem* is a *team problem*, here are some questions to consider:

> ➤ *Have team members accepted their stewardship, or area of responsibility, and are they duly empowered, i.e. are they being engaged as "partners" rather than "employees," with all that such implies?*

> ➤ *Are team members correctly placed according to their talents, strengths and interests?*

> ➤ *Do team members understand and appreciate the importance of their contribution, and the expected results they have committed to deliver?*

> ➤ *Are they being developed to think critically and creatively and to solve complex problems developmentally and collaboratively?*

> ➤ *Are they well trained in key processes?*

> ➤ *Is store management creating an environment in which partners and associates are accountable by choice for their performance and the results they achieve?*

> ➤ *Is the company, through all layers of management, contributing to optimal performance through collaborative-based approaches to management? Or is it undermining empowerment, commitment, and high performance through control-based management approaches that spawn and mobilize personal and organizational defenses?*

These and similar questions are grappled with in subsequent chapters. We have found that because of their nature and implications, they cannot easily be answered either honestly or factually. Rather, they are topics for continual introspection, action research and cultural assessment within the organization.

At the third level of the Problem Pyramid, *people* are the root of a *presenting problem*. The *presenting problem* occurs because the team is not effectively executing or performing. The team is not properly implementing established processes that are in place to ensure that the store runs effectively and achieves the desired results. Programs and systems are not being followed consistently, and the results are not being achieved because of a performance problem somewhere in the team.

In some cases, *team problems* are truly team-oriented, meaning that the entire team, or a large part of the team, suffers from the same core problem, which leads to substandard performance overall. An example might be a store team that feels defeated due to consistent failure, constant turnover or oppressive, neglectful leadership. Another example might be a team that has been recently formed, where team members are new to each other and their roles and have not completed the necessary "storming," "norming," and "performing" cycles. In such cases, one could reasonably expect to find inconsistent performance and erratic execution.

*Team problems* may also stem from specific problems with individual team members - a lack of engagement, for example, or an attitude of compliance, rather than internal commitment, made worse by unacknowledged resistance to change and/or the absence of sufficient individual involvement in resolving problems and improving performance.

## MANAGEMENT PROBLEMS

If we need processes to ensure that store conditions are at the appropriate level, and we need a team to execute those processes effectively, who is responsible for ensuring that a capable store team is in place and being upgraded as necessary to provide the consistent achievement of targeted results?

The answer leads us to the root source of all problems in the store: the store manager. *Management problems stem from the store manager's failure to consistently deliver expected store results at or above plan and brand requirements.* This failure is due, in turn, to the store manager's inability and/or unwillingness to continuously and effectively build and upgrade a high-performance store team by:

1. *hiring the right people and placing them in the right positions according to their attitude, values, talents, strengths, experience, skills and knowledge;*

2. *retaining the right people according to the criteria for hiring above and for actual performance and degree of engagement;*

3. *promoting the right people on the basis of all the criteria for retention above and readiness and willingness for advancement;*

4. *replacing or removing, without delay, those who don't fulfill expectations or are not contributing;*

5. *developing each member of the store executive team and associates through ongoing partnering and learning.*

Some questions for field executives to consider in relation to *management problems* in the store include:

> ➤ *Have we hired, appointed, retained, or promoted the right person to be the store manager? On the basis of what criteria?*

> ➤ *Is the store manager truly engaged? How do we know? What does such engagement look like behaviorally?*

> ➤ *Is the store manager building and upgrading his team? What evidence supports this?*

> ➤ *Does he have the talent, strengths and skills to do that? How do we know?*

> ➤ *Does he have the commitment and desire? How do we know? What does such commitment look like behaviorally?*

> ➤ *Does he have the knowledge of the business necessary to run the store and achieve targeted results? How do we know?*

> ➤ *Is he effective at ensuring that the team is continuously being built, managed, and upgraded, and that operating problems are being identified and solved, and at the right level? What's the evidence?*

Upgrading the team is a core responsibility in the role of any manager - a store manager, a DM or a VP. Again, to build and upgrade his team effectively, a manager, at any level, must be doing five things on an ongoing and consistent basis. He or she must:

> ➤ *hire and place the right people in the right roles;*

> ➤ *remove (and possibly even terminate the employment of) those people who turn out not to be right;*

> ➤ *retain the right people;*

> ➤ *promote the right people;*

> ➤ *develop people through ongoing partnering and learning.*

To elaborate a bit further, the "right" people to hire are those who share company values in important areas, such as teamwork, customer focus, development and work ethic. They are placed in terms of their personalities, natural talents, personal strengths, skills, will, and attitude toward the vision of the organization.

The "right" people to retain are team members who demonstrate the values, priorities and standards of the business, as evidenced by their consistently effective behavior and performance. These are the team members who are internally committed, engaged, teachable, and accountable by choice.

The "right" team members to promote are those who have additionally demonstrated a willingness and capacity to assume greater responsibility and a desire and capability to learn and develop.

The "right" people to remove, through transfer, repositioning or termination of employment, are those who are not performing effectively or who will not own their attitudes, behavior and results, or who stubbornly resist change or are complacent or satisfied with a less than acceptable level of performance.

The *management problem* as defined above is the highest leverage problem in any given store at any given time. A DM visiting a store might find dozens of *presenting problems*, problems that have very likely been identified and addressed multiple times, yet continue to recur. Underneath such *presenting problems* are processes, routines, systems, and programs that aren't being executed correctly, or are perhaps faulty. They're not being executed correctly or improved because of team performance problems. And team performance problems point to a store manager who is not effectively building and upgrading his team. Thus, the root cause of every recurring *presenting problem* in any store is, in the final analysis, the store manager. All problems are in the end, *management problems*.

In looking carefully at the anatomy of a problem, the DM or VP needs to focus on the deepest level, the root of performance problems – the management. The VPs need to concentrate on their DMs' development and performance in building and upgrading their district management teams and the DMs need to stay focused on their store managers' development and performance in building and upgrading their district store management teams. They need to stay focused on the store manager, not on the *presenting problems*, not on the *process problems*, and not on the people or *team problems*. The store manager owns that store and is responsible for store conditions, making his numbers, ensuring customer satisfaction, all through an effective store team. The store manager is responsible for building and upgrading a store team that executes the programs and processes that bring about desired results.

The DM's *highest point of leverage* in creating an optimally performing district is to focus on whether his store managers have the skills, knowledge, character strength and desire to build and upgrade their respective teams. Specifically, the DM's role is to determine whether or not the store manager knows how to facilitate reflective and collaborative learning and problem solving and partner with his managers to establish baseline empowerment and accountability. Once he is certain of that, his role is to develop that store manager in the areas he is deficient and ultimately to upgrade the district store management team as needed. The VP's and the DM's role is *not* to help that store manager solve *presenting and process problems* as they walk through the store, or even *team problems* when they occur. While such assistance might be indicated briefly in stores with new, inexperienced store managers or in cases where the store is in crisis, it is not indicated on a continuous, periodic or long-term basis.

In solving a store performance problem the focus must be on the *right problem*, at the *right level*, in order to address the root cause of the problem and prevent its recurrence. The reason that the same presenting problems come up, within the same teams, in the same stores, over and over again, is that field executives are focused on solving *them* rather focusing on the underlying *management problems*.

What we should be seeing in the field is the visiting VP focusing on how effectively the DM is focusing on the store manager's ability to identify and solve team performance problems and to build and upgrade his store management team accordingly. This means that, in addressing execution problems in the stores, the DM needs to be able to effectively assess store management performance and design and test developmental field interventions that accomplish two objectives:

> **OBJECTIVE #1:** *Develop the store manager's ability to address team performance problems consistently and effectively by building and upgrading the store team; and*

> **OBJECTIVE #2:** *Produce valid information regarding the store manager's ability and desire in building and upgrading the store team in order to determine what changes, if any, need to be made to build and upgrade the district store management team.*

What we see in the field, however, is just the opposite. Our research shows that between *90 and 95 percent* of a typical VP/DM store visit is spent focusing on *presenting problems*, which is the *lowest leverage point of change*. In other words, VPs and DMs are spending 90 to 95 percent of their time focusing on the *wrong problems*. Between three and five percent of their time is spent on *process problems* and the remainder of the time, if any, is spent in perfunctory conversation on the team and the expectations of the store manager.

This is very different from what *every* VP and DM we interviewed before he went into the field told us he planned on doing once he got there. In *every case*, there was a significant gap between how the field executives intended to act and how they actually acted. None of the executives disagreed with the need for a developmental focus on the store manager as the root problem, but all focused on the *presenting problems*.

It became clear through the research that the way the VPs and DMs were visiting the stores was, in fact, a significant part of the problem and characterized their own *skilled incompetence*. It also became evident that in certain retail organizations such skilled incompetence was being compensated for and covered up by the creation of additional infrastructure - new staff support positions and ad hoc store support teams in the field designed to 'jump start' poor or marginally performing stores.

Such structural strategies are clearly defensive in nature and evidence of a deeply embedded defensive orientation. They fail to address the skilled incompetence of field executives and thereby perpetuate the underlying problem at the heart of inconsistent store performance.

What would the time allocation need to look like if the DM was focused on the right problems at the store level?

You're correct if you noted that the numbers would be inverted. The DM would be spending 90 to 95 percent of his time in development conversations with the store manager to determine the health and condition of the team and the needs of the manager in developing and upgrading the store team.

The vast majority – in excess of 90 percent – of the DM's time should be spent focusing on the store manager's commitment performance and development.

We will return in Chapter 5 to the question of how store visits would actually look if field executives truly focused on the root *management problem* and embraced a collaborative, learning-based developmental approach to store improvement instead of the prevailing control-based IDC approach presented in the previous chapter.

At this point, we want to conclude by addressing the second part of the dilemma affecting store performance: the problem of speed.

## SPEED AND THE TIME MANAGEMENT PROBLEM

Most of the field executives we work with today feel as though they are under a tremendous amount of pressure to make everything happen quickly. With competitive pressures and corporate demands looming, they feel they don't have the time to do the job the way they believe it should be done. Many see lack of time as the primary impediment in their ability to get everything done that needs to get done in order to create the results that are expected of them.

One group of field executives convinced themselves that they needed a course in time management. We agreed to meet and work with them, though with a strong suspicion that their problem wasn't lack of time; their problem was how they were spending their time.

If the DM is spending his time in the stores addressing *presenting problems*, he is focusing on problems at the wrong level. The core issues are not getting addressed. The problems will only get bigger, and both the field executive and the store manager will be spending an inordinate amount of time in a crisis mode.

By working on the right problem, at the bottom of the problem pyramid, the field executive will realize that his "time management" problem is not really a time problem at all.

When we first met with the group of retail field executives who were convinced they had a "time management" problem, we asked them to make a detailed list of all the things they were responsible for accomplishing on a day-to-day basis. Then we asked, "How many of the items on this list do you do on your own?"

"None of it," they replied.

"Can you do all of this by yourself?"

"No, of course not."

"Who do you need to get this list accomplished?

"We need people."

"Right. You need your team. And the store manager needs his team.

"If you really want to make time for yourself, why are you trying to do your store managers' jobs? Why aren't you focusing on developing them so that they will be truly empowered and choose to be accountable for doing what they're supposed to be doing? If they are engaged in learning and in doing what they've committed to do, you won't have to constantly check up on them and do it for them. How will that impact your time dilemma?"

They got it. The next hurdle was their realization that they didn't know how to truly develop their people. They didn't know how to partner with their store managers to foster empowerment and accountability or how to facilitate the kind of learning that resulted in lasting and ongoing improvement. Those skills we could help them with.

The point is "time management" is rarely about lack of time. It's often about the way an executive is misusing that time. Don't be seduced into believing that your real problem is merely a lack of time.

## THE HARDER AND FASTER YOU WORK, THE QUICKER YOU SINK

In the movie *The Replacements*, a group of amateur football players were brought into the professional league to replace the pro players who were out on strike. Keanu Reeves was the quarterback of the replacement team. In a team meeting in the midst of training, the coach, played by Gene Hackman, asked the players what they were afraid of. "What are your fears?" he asked. "We must come to terms with our fears."

"Quicksand," Reeves' character said. His teammates didn't understand. He explained that you're playing the game, and you're playing hard, and you make a mistake. You know you made it. You get anxious and try harder so that you don't make another one. Then you make another mistake. You try harder yet. The harder you try, the more mistakes you make. Pretty soon you realize you are sinking. It's like being in quicksand. The harder you try to get out, the more it drags you under.

The image of quicksand is a good metaphor for the speed trap in business. Very often, the more time you put in, the harder you work, and the faster you work, the faster you sink.

The story is told about a person getting lost on his way to a meeting. He's driving along, using the map he was given, trying to figure out exactly where he's supposed to be going. He realizes he's running late, so he starts driving a little faster. Unfortunately, the faster he drives, the more lost he becomes. That, naturally, brings about frustration. He decides there's only so much he can do, so he needs to let go of the frustration and adopt a positive attitude. The next thing he knows, he's even more lost, but he has a better attitude about it.

In this person's case, the map he was following was wrong. If you have a wrong map, even if you double your efforts and adopt a positive attitude, you'll only manage to get lost twice as fast, albeit with a smile on your face. Attitude is not the problem. Time is not the problem. It's the map. Speed and a positive attitude don't help if you're focused on addressing the *wrong* problems, or even the right problems the *wrong* way.

If you're focusing on the wrong problems (the *presenting problems*) with the wrong approach (the inspect/direct/correct approach) you're almost certain to find yourself in quicksand. The faster you go, the harder you try, the more you extend your days and weeks to visit more and more stores, the faster you will sink.

A field executive who complains that he doesn't have enough time in the day is almost certainly not building and upgrading his team effectively. The more he personally addresses the same recurring problems with his IDC approach, the more he is fostering inconsistent execution, anti-learning, defensiveness, dependency, and a total breakdown of accountability. As a result, the same recurring problems keep right on occurring. Why? Because they have not been addressed at the right level in the right way, and thus have not been solved. Working out of the IDC model, what does this executive do in response to the recurring problems? He gets up earlier in the morning, visits two extra stores each day, creates more checklists for store managers, doubles his efforts and works at a faster pace.

What happens? He sinks.

If you want speed, which is absolutely essential in today's competitive retail environment, and you're not getting the results you want and need on a consistent basis because the team isn't performing or executing effectively, then *you have to slow down.* You have to slow down and focus on the right problem in a radically different way that takes time. You have to focus on the right problem in a way that promotes the development of your people through empowerment, learning and accountability.

Clearly, our "If you want speed, you have to slow down" advice is challenging in today's business environment, which is all about getting results NOW. But one thing is certain: the current fast-paced, control-based approach is not consistently producing targeted results. It is simply not working, if working means consistently achieving and exceeding standards and plan in all parts of our stores. We try harder and things don't improve, or if they do improve, the improvement is not ongoing and results are inconsistent and/or sub-optimal over time.

The fact is development takes time. Empowerment through partnering requires the carefully negotiated release of control and power, and that takes time. Reflective, design-based learning takes time. Solving the right problems in the right way takes time. Achieving high performance takes time. Improving store performance takes time. Anyone who suggests otherwise is simply in denial or just plain wrong.

What's needed, besides a re-visioning of the role and contribution of store support functions, which we will address in Chapter 5, is a radically different approach to field leadership and a radically different mindset.

Over time, as your developmental efforts begin to pay off, team members will begin to think through problems on their own and solve them at the appropriate level. As a result, their sense of commitment increases and they become personally accountable by choice for their performance. The wise investment of your time begins to pay off. You are no longer addressing the same *presenting problems* with the same people again and again. You are working at the right level, building and upgrading your regional, district or store management teams, which then become accountable for their results.

If you are a retail field executive, given the focus suggested in this chapter, imagine how your store visits might be different. What would such a change assume? What would it look like structurally and behaviorally? How would you personally need to change? What would keep you from making such needed changes? Again, these questions will be answered in Chapters 4 and 5.

In the next chapter we will explore the root causes of failed execution in the retail environment. We will also present what we think is the missing Leadership Factor for producing consistently great store performance, a factor consisting of the dynamic interplay of three fundamentals of effective execution. This Leadership Factor is the *developmental lever* that will lead to great store performance. It is the basis for effectively resolving the "root" problem impeding great store performance; the missing ingredient we need to restore in order to solve the right store problems in the right way.

## KEY INSIGHTS FROM CHAPTER 2:

➤ *Field executives are addressing the wrong problems in the wrong way and don't know it.*

➤ *They are speeding up ineffectively, which is slowing them down.*

➤ *They think they have a lack of time to get it all done, but their problem is how they're spending their time, not that there isn't enough of it.*

➤ *They're trying to solve 100 presenting problems at 1%, instead of 1 root problem at 100%.*

➤ *The incorrect approach to leading ensures that the presenting problems will continue to recur and results will be sub-optimal and inconsistent.*

➤ *Field executives need to:*

   ▪ *Slow down.*

   ▪ *Focus on the right problem, at the right level, in the right way.*

   ▪ *Spend the vast majority of store visit time focusing on the store manager's performance, his ability to focus on his own problems at the right level, and how he's upgrading his team to enable consistent, on-target performance.*

# CHAPTER 3

# INCONSISTENT STORE PERFORMANCE: THE MISSING LEADERSHIP FACTOR

*In this chapter:*

➢ *Why is consistently effective execution in stores so elusive?*

➢ *Can we realistically expect store manager and associate engagement, internal commitment, and accountability without empowerment and continuous learning?*

➢ *Can there be real empowerment when there is little or no risk, autonomy or uncertainty in the roles of the store manager or associate, or when there is no real partnership between managers and direct reports?*

➢ *Can there be true performance accountability without the voluntary choice of ownership?*

➢ *How can there be personal change without unlearning what isn't working through the constructive exposure of error?*

We now know that the primary reason we repeatedly experience the same problems in stores (Dilemma #1) is that we're focused on solving the *wrong problems*. This is so in spite of all the experience and talent in our organizations and in spite of the numerous times we've seemingly solved these same problems.

Once we're focused on the correct problem, at the right level of the Problem Pyramid, we can tackle Dilemma #2: *why are we unable to consistently achieve targeted results?*

The second dilemma builds on the first. Solving the dilemma of inconsistent performance requires that we focus at the Team and Management levels of the Problem Pyramid. These are the two deepest levels, where the complex and high leverage performance problems reside. Here, by focusing primarily on the store manager and, through the store manager, on the store team, we can more clearly understand the complexities of the issues and design potential solutions that have a greater opportunity to resolve the problems, once and for all.

## FAILED EXECUTION

Failure to achieve targeted results is a failure of execution. When this happens, the store manager and his or her team members are not appropriately executing in one or more of several key areas. They might not be fully engaged or clear about what's expected. They might not have the tools, resources, or training to accomplish what's expected, or are not learning how to better deal with complex problems to deliver what's expected. They might be poised defensively between competing commitments and priorities or stuck in a position that doesn't play to their talents or strengths. Or, they just might not care, and there is not a culture of accountability that calls them to perform according to expectations.

All of these problems are examples of Team and Management level problems. But how do you know which specific problems are at play? And once you know, how do you address them? These problems are complex and intermingled. In our experience, they are most successfully addressed when seen and approached through the lens of three fundamental ideas: *Empowerment, Accountability,* and *Learning.* The dynamic interdependence of these three fundamentals comprises what we refer to as the "Leadership Factor" of development.

## THE MISSING LEADERSHIP FACTOR

The Leadership Factor has been conspicuous by its absence in nearly every store visit and interaction we have observed over the years. It is missing in part because the ideas and practice of empowerment, accountability, and learning have lost their usefulness and power due to overuse, misuse or misunderstanding.

In a word, the Leadership Factor is about development, another misunderstood and misused term. Development is not synonymous with training, teaching or coaching, or with learning new skills or techniques. It is not an activity, program or event. It is, rather, a progressive and sustained change of orientation, attitude, motivation and behavior.

Work related development is evident when someone becomes truly accountable and internally committed to his work; when, as both Peter

Block and Peter Senge suggest, the person becomes a partner who owns the vision, who will make it happen, creating whatever systems, policies, and changes are necessary to make it happen. All, we might add, without the need for supervision, permission, external recognition, "happy talk," or material incentives.

Further, work related development is evident when the orientation to action shifts from being predominantly defensive to being more collaborative. The first orientation, which we address in Chapter 4, is characterized by various forms of self-protective, face-saving behavior and control-based approaches to action. It is also characterized, hearkening back to the work of Eric Berne, by various dysfunctional "parent/child," "parent/parent," and "child/child" transaction patterns between and among bosses and subordinates. It is reactive and primarily self-aggrandizing and self-protective in nature.

The second orientation to action, which we will present in Chapter 5, is characterized by collaborative behavior, critical thinking, reflective learning and problem solving. It is also characterized by mature "adult/adult" interaction patterns respecting diversity, inclusion, mutual benefit, voluntary choice, dissent, and creative negotiation. It is self-reflective and primarily developmental in nature.

Finally, the move in development is from externally derived motivation, which is minimal and short-lived at best, to internal commitment, which is derived by personal success through creative learning and self-directed action. Such change is best facilitated, in our experience, in two ways: first, by placing the team member or manager in the right role according to his or her talents, strengths and interests; and second, by applying the Leadership Factor. Of these two ways to productive change, we think the second way is primary.

While placement is clearly important, it is not decisive as a facilitator of productive change in performance and is certainly not sufficient. A person can be properly placed according to natural talents and strengths and not perform well. This happens all the time. The converse is also true. People can perform well in roles that do not necessarily play to their strengths.

What is decisive is the conscious transitioning of orientation, attitude, action and behavior, which can be accomplished to a sufficient degree through the correct and continual application of the Leadership Factor.

This chapter will provide a necessary conceptual foundation of the three fundamental ideas comprising the Leadership Factor of development. Chapter 5 will incorporate them in a new, developmental approach to retail field management that aims to resolve all three dilemmas and facilitate great store performance.

# FIGURE 3:
## THE LEADERSHIP FACTOR OF DEVELOPMENT

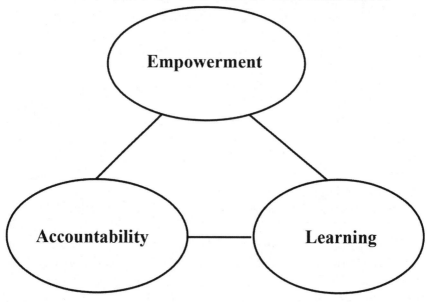

## MISCONCEPTIONS, MISUNDERSTANDINGS AND MISUSES

There are a multitude of varying definitions for the words empowerment, accountability and learning. The most common, in the retail sector, are as follows:

> ➤ *Empowerment has come to be a catch-all word for assigning responsibility, usually through a job description at the date of hire. For some it entails giving subordinates the training, direction and tools they need to do their job. Empowerment also means encouraging others, usually through persuasion, recognition and incentive, to take the initiative and the risk to do whatever it takes (within policy and reason) to get desired results. These very limited understandings of empowerment rarely, if ever, result in employee commitment, engagement, accountability, or world-class performance for reasons that will soon become evident.*

➤ *Accountability is typically, and erroneously, viewed as an issue related to authority: "You are accountable for..." or "You, as the store manager, must hold your people accountable." In this line of thinking, the employee is technically accountable to the company and his manager by virtue of taking the job and collecting a paycheck. It is the store manager's job to make sure the employee, or associate, is doing the job he's getting paid to do, and doing it right. By checking up on employees and continually providing direction, directives and feedback, you will get them to perform, leave or get fired. This flawed understanding is based on an erroneous belief and assumption. First, executives and managers wrongly believe that world-class performance and accountability can be mandated and enforced. Second, they wrongly assume that employees are naturally accountable because they collect a paycheck or merely because they say they are accountable.*

➤ *Learning commonly means acquiring a new idea or insight through experience or formal education. In an organization, learning is often equated with the acquisition of new skills or information as the result of training, coaching, modeling and directing. The flawed assumption here is that if people are taught, told, or shown what to do, they will learn how to do their job and they'll do it right. This might hold with certain simple, procedural tasks, but not for dealing effectively with more complex performance problems that require more involved or sophisticated interactive approaches.*

We urge you to set aside whatever preconceptions you may have about the words *empowerment, accountability* and *learning.* Our definitions of these terms are different and specific, as is our approach. It is critical to understanding our approach that you understand these terms as we are using them and see how different our definitions are from others.

## RE-DEFINING THE INDIVIDUAL ELEMENTS OF THE LEADERSHIP FACTOR

*Empowerment,* as we see it, entails the conferral and voluntary acceptance of an area of responsibility, or a *stewardship.* Such a stewardship usually takes the form of a particular position or role and comes with a commitment and obligation to perform according to mutually understood and accepted responsibilities, guidelines and expectations. Empowerment is the fruit of a genuine, formal partnership between a manager and direct report.

*Accountability* is the reporting partner's self-imposed commitment to "own" and honor the terms and conditions of the stewardship, or partnership agreement. To own in this sense is to be accountable by free and informed choice. *Performance Accountability* is born when both partners get to "yes" through honest collaboration and creative negotiation. It occurs when the reporting partner can essentially say with sufficient conviction, "Yes, I accept the terms of this partnership as being reasonable and achievable." In this sense, accountability means personal commitment, being responsible, *by choice*, for delivering the desired and agreed-upon results. Empowerment and accountability are, therefore, interdependent. Through true empowerment a person becomes accountable.

*Learning* occurs when we discover the inadequacies of our approaches to action and design better approaches that will result in more consistently effective performance. It occurs when we detect and correct error, or the gap between intended and actual performance. Learning also occurs when we first experience a match between intentions and results. Learning is related to both action and results and is continually evolving, as situations dictate, through ongoing action research and design. It is the outcome of working collaboratively with others to research and design more effective ways to achieve targeted results. It entails "unlearning" as a necessary prerequisite and rigorous analysis and testing as essential requirements for new learning. Such reflective, design-based learning, as distinguished from skill-based or experience-based learning, will be presented later in this chapter. Suffice to say, it is indispensable, along with empowerment and accountability, in achieving great store performance through consistently effective execution.

In the sections that follow, we will go beyond the revised definitions above and revisit each element of the Leadership Factor in more depth and in relation to each other as they apply to the achievement of great store performance.

## EMPOWERMENT THROUGH PARTNERSHIP

For baseline empowerment to exist in a relationship between, say, a DM and a store manager, both parties must first be completely clear and in agreement regarding the terms, conditions and requirements of the partnership. This would include the store manager's *role* and related core *responsibilities*, as well as *objectives* to be accomplished in each of the store's key result areas. It would also include specified *decision rights*, or levels of authority, inherent in the core responsibilities. Additionally, it would include a delineation of necessary *resources* and those (very) few non-negotiable *operating guidelines* established by company policy. Finally, there would need to be a solid, mutual understanding of the processes, measurements and mechanisms of accounting for performance and the consequences of performance, or non-performance.

The notion of stewardship is an important aspect of empowerment that warrants some elaboration. Peter Block explores the idea of stewardship perhaps more thoroughly than anyone else in his book *Stewardship: Choosing Service Over Self-Interest* (1993, Berrett-Koehler). In his book, Block explains operating in a stewardship as governing ourselves in a way that creates a strong sense of *ownership* and *responsibility for outcomes*. It is operating with a sense of accountability for those outcomes without all the controls that are intended to create compliance, and that result in an environment of dependency and underperformance. For Block, the role of the supervisor, or "managing partner," is better seen as a "supplier" or "banker" to the reporting partner, rather than as a "customer."

Empowerment, Block says, is the belief that the answers to our most pressing and complex problems can usually be resolved at the level of the organization closest to the problem, those with the specific expertise necessary.

Dependency, in contrast, rests on the belief that it is the people in power, the managers, who know what should be done, and we should look to them for the answers. In a dependent culture, the employees look to the leaders to make decisions and create an environment where they can live a life of safety and predictability. We refer to this as a "parental" environment, where employees operate essentially as children, subservient to their parent's direction.

As we mentioned, in order for baseline empowerment and performance accountability to flourish there must be an environment of adult partnership rather than a traditional supervisor-subordinate relationship. In a partnership, each party is accountable to the other and to the company for the delivery of an agreed upon outcome. There is a mutual investment in each other's and the company's success. The primary motivation of partnership is achievement, and its governing principles are service, collaboration and mutual ownership and accountability.

In order to operate as partners, there must be clarity around the essential elements of the partnership and a true release of power and control. To accomplish this, we advocate working together to create what we call the *Performance Partnership Agreement (PPA)*. This is a commitment between two partners that spells out the substance and structure of the delegated stewardship. Throughout this chapter and in various places in this book we refer to the PPA as both an oral agreement and a written agreement. From our perspective, the PPA is, first and foremost, the mutually understood and accepted verbal understanding between two partners. The written notes of the agreement are reminders for each partner of his or her respective commitment to the other in the context of organizational requirements.

The process of creating the agreement is designed to stimulate open dialogue between the parties. The PPA establishes the baseline empowerment of the direct report, whom we refer to as the "reporting partner," and initiates performance accountability on the part of both partners to each other. The essential elements of such an agreement, once again, include:

> ➤ *The reporting partner's role and specific responsibilities in the larger context of the organization's mission, vision, brand promise and core values, strategies, policies and financial goals.*

> ➤ *The types of decisions they make and their corresponding level of authority.*

> ➤ *The specific expectations of their performance, meaning the results they're responsible for delivering.*

> ➤ *The operating guidelines, policies or other "non-negotiable" parameters that govern their role.*

> ➤ *The resources that can be made available to them, as needed.*

> ➤ *The required terms and measurements of reporting accountability and the likely consequences, both positive and negative, to the organization as well as both partners personally, resulting from their performance.*

The Performance Partnership Agreement is as symbolic as it is practical. Symbolically it connotes the move from parental supervision and the corresponding defensive orientation to a relationship characterized by adult interaction through mutually respectful collaboration and negotiation.

Practically, the written agreement gives both partners a tool for monitoring their own performances and accounting to each other on progress and results. The agreement clarifies, in very specific terms, the stewardship that is being invested in the individual and serves as the basis for balancing the needs for release and control.

Equally important is what the PPA process and written agreement are *not*. The process is *not* a control-based exercise designed to help the manager exert *control* over the direct report and the environment. It is a *collaborative* process that results in, at minimum, a 75 percent consensus between both parties. This means that each person can honestly say, in effect, "75% of me feels this agreement is both reasonable and achievable." The agreement is, of course, limited by company policies and financial plans imposed from the top down onto the store's organization. Still, both partners work creatively within corporate guidelines and requirements to come to a mutually acceptable understanding that is both reasonable and achievable. This is difficult work that takes time, care and due diligence.

In addition, the formal agreement is not necessarily a legally binding employment agreement. Nor is it merely a job description. While some clients have adopted the written PPA in lieu of job descriptions and used them as addendums to employment agreements or as source documents for their performance appraisal and management system, it is not mandatory to use it in these ways.

The process for creating the actual partnership agreement is not presented here because its application requires specialized training in the skills of collaboration (presented later in this chapter) and creative negotiation. Also, in most cases, the process is best facilitated, in most cases, by an external expert to ensure that both partners get to real consensus in their negotiations.

To better understand the nature and power of such partnering we need to take a deeper look at each of the elements of the PPA.

## THE ESSENTIAL ELEMENTS OF THE PPA

The PPA has several key elements, each of which plays an important role in establishing baseline empowerment and accountability within the delegated stewardship. What follows is an elaboration of the eight suggested elements of the partnership agreement arranged in a hypothetical PPA between a DM and a store manager.

## 1. ROLE AND CONTRIBUTION

This first element of the agreement defines the reporting partner's role - what the partner is actually charged with doing.

For a store manager position, the role could look something like this:

*The role in the position of Store Manager is to optimize store performance at all levels of the store, as set forth in this Partnership Agreement. The Store Manager is charged, first and foremost, with the responsibility for continuously building and upgrading a high-performance store team as needed, and on an ongoing basis to ensure the consistent achievement of expected results through consistently effective execution. This store is the Store Manager's stewardship, or area of responsibility. By optimizing store performance as required, the Store Manager contributes to the overall success of this district, region, and of the company as a whole.*

## 2. RESPONSIBILITIES

This element of the agreement establishes, very specifically, each of the actions the person should take in order to fulfill his or her role. It is not necessary to capture every small responsibility or task. The agreement should capture those critical few responsibilities related to the key result areas of the store.

## EXAMPLE:

*The Store Manager is responsible for:*

➢ *Maintaining store conditions and customer service levels according to the standards related to the vision and brand promise of the organization.*

➢ *Consistently meeting or exceeding plan in every financial category.*

➢ *Building and continually upgrading a high performance store management team, consisting of an assistant store manager and individual department managers, who are sufficiently trained and developed to manage their functional areas of responsibility and achieve their specific, targeted results.*

➢ *Strategically managing store space to optimize sales and enhance the customers' shopping experience.*

➢ *Operating the store consistent with the company's health and safety standards and ensuring employee safety as a top priority in every department.*

## 3. MEASURABLE EXPECTATIONS / DELIVERABLES

Ultimately, it is impossible to measure success if there is nothing to measure, so expected deliverable results should be clearly defined wherever possible. In this element of the agreement, those deliverables, which govern the role, are spelled out in specific terms. These will typically include financial goals or sales targets in total and by category, customer service scores, payroll costs, departmental expenses, gross and net profits, spoilage, shrinkage, and other relevant performance standards.

In establishing such expectations, great care should be taken to avoid sending crippling mixed messages. For example, instead of the stated expectation requiring store managers to, say, "focus on improving and sustaining associate engagement, not the numbers," which sets up a mixed message through either/or thinking, consider the revised expectation to "focus on *both* the improvement and sustaining of associate engagement *and* results." This second expectation, which focuses on results *through* associate engagement, is the product of both/and thinking, rather than either/or thinking.

## EXAMPLE:

(note: wherever a specific item states "as defined," that detail should be included or attached to the agreement so that there is no confusion around expected performance):

➢ *Meeting or exceeding budgeted/targeted financial and operational results, as follows:*

-- *Period sales targets, as defined.*

> *-- Period expense and profitability targets, as defined.*
>
> *-- Customer satisfaction scores, as defined.*
>
> *-- Maximum shrinkage targets, as defined.*
>
> *--Staffing and upgrading the team as needed and defined.*

> ➢ *Meeting period employee safety incident targets, as defined.*

> ➢ *Maintaining store conditions consistent with Brand, as defined.*

> ➢ *Focus on improving and sustaining associate engagement and commitment in your store toward the consistent achievement of plan.*

> ➢ *Executing all storewide merchandising programs consistent with plans and timelines.*

## 4. POLICIES, GUIDELINES AND OTHER OPERATING PARAMETERS

With all roles come an assortment of policies, guidelines and other specific operating parameters. These include company policies and procedures, regional or district-specific policies, and laws or other applicable regulations. In almost every case, these are the non-negotiable restrictions that govern a role. There should be as few as possible and listed in this section of the agreement. *The rule is simple: the longer the list of non-negotiable operating guidelines, the less the empowerment.* For simplicity, these guidelines may be incorporated by reference, where appropriate. In some cases, for particular emphasis, it may be important to detail them more specifically.

**EXAMPLE:**

The Store Manager is responsible for ensuring compliance with the following:

> ➢ *The policies and standard operating procedures of the company, as defined.*

> ➢ *The company's "Brand Standards", as defined.*

> ➢ *Applicable federal and state health and safety regulations, as defined.*

> ➢ *All appropriate federal, state and local statutes, as defined.*

## 5. DECISION TYPES AND RIGHTS (LEVELS OF AUTHORITY)

Inherent in the responsibilities of any given role are recurring types of decisions that must be made and executed on a routine basis in order to effectively discharge such responsibilities. This element of the PPA includes those decisions that are defined and categorized into specific *decision types*. Then, they are assigned the *levels of authority* the partner has in making these types of decisions. The level of authority granted is the *decision right*.

This process is intended to take away any ambiguity about the decisions that need to be made and the authority the person has in making them. It is also intended to balance the tension between release and control by addressing the need for consistency in delivering the brand promise through the progressive escalation of decision rights. This balance can be achieved through effective partnering rather than through the imposition of additional infrastructure and controls.

The levels of authority granted to different associates may differ, even if those associates are in the same job. They should be jointly set and then periodically reviewed and adjusted, based upon both partners' level of confidence in the reporting partner's ability to make effective decisions. For those who are newer to a role or inexperienced, authority levels can be set at a lower level in the initial stages of the relationship with the expectation that they will be re-evaluated and raised to a higher level as they demonstrate their ability to make sound decisions and achieve expected results.

There are three levels of authority that will govern all of these decisions. They are as follows, together with corresponding guidelines:

## LEVEL 1

➤ *Act only after consultation with the DM.*

➤ *DM retains veto power over this decision.*

➤ *Store manager retains responsibility for the decision and is still accountable for the outcome, but in the event of a veto by the DM, must develop an alternative, acceptable solution.*

## LEVEL 2

➤ *Act after soliciting input and feedback with the DM and, if applicable, other experts or parties who might be affected by the decision.*

➤ *Decision is the store manager's to make*

➤ *DM cannot veto, but is given the opportunity to be involved in the discussion and have views considered prior to the action.*

## LEVEL 3

➤ *Act unilaterally and advise or inform DM, as appropriate, after taking action*

➤ *Decision is the store manager's to make*

➤ *Store manager is expected to make decisions on the basis of valid information and sound judgment and to solicit, receive and consider any input appropriate to the decision before taking action.*

➤ *This is not a license to make decisions on the sole basis of personal preference or in a vacuum.*

## EXAMPLE:

| | |
|---|---|
| *Associate Hiring Decisions* | *Level 3* |
| *Associate Terminations/Transfers* | *Level 3* |
| *Department Manager Hiring Decisions* | *Level 2* |
| *Department Manager Terminations/Transfers* | *Level 2* |
| *Alteration of Store Space Layout and* | |
|       *Merchandising Plan-O-Grams* | *Level 2* |
| *Expenditures < $1,000* | *Level 3* |
| *Expenditures > $1,000* | *Level 1* |

## 6. NEEDED RESOURCES

In many instances, in order for an individual to deliver results consistent with expectations, an individual requires some level of additional resources or development to augment his or her expertise, skill set or capabilities. This is a natural and important part of individual growth. People who are actively engaged in development become more accountable and receptive to growth and change and, by a large margin, perform at or above expectation.

To establish this element of the agreement, the store manager and DM collectively identify specific opportunities to increase the direct report's capability to deliver results through development or the application of additional resources. Once defined and agreed upon, the DM will take responsibility for supplying or approving the required resources, as appropriate. Such items could include personalized leadership coaching for the store manager or other team members around a specific technical discipline, or other requirements, as indicated by the specific situation.

## EXAMPLE:

➢ *DM to provide staff and expense budgets according to plan and special need, as approved.*

➢ *Store manager to attend "Advance Store Management" course, provided by Corporate Training, within the next six months.*

➢ *Store manager to attend three-day "Finance and Accounting for Non-financial Managers" course at local community college. Time off and expenses to be provided by the company.*

> ➤ *DM to dedicate one day a month for the next six months to work with store manager as a personal coach specifically focused on increasing the store manager's abilities in the area of store team development.*

> ➤ *DM to conduct developmental store visits on an ongoing basis, using the Observe/Inquire/Develop Approach, not the Inspect/ Direct/Correct Approach.*

## 7. BEHAVIORAL GUIDELINES

The next step in the PPA process is establishing some of the key behavioral guidelines that will govern the relationship between partners. How difficult this part of the process is depends on the history of the relationship and how comfortable they are addressing sensitive issues. It requires a high level of maturity and honesty. It might be necessary to have an experienced facilitator involved in this stage, particularly in a strained or troubled relationship.

Each partner defines specific, observable behaviors that they request their partner either stop doing, start doing, or continue doing, in order to support them in the fulfillment of their end of the partnership agreement. These points should be as specific and observable as possible for clarity. There will likely be at least a few items in each of the three (stop/start/ continue) columns. If not, it's reasonable to question the honesty of the partner who can't seem to think of anything. The average agreement between two individuals who have experience working with one another contains between 15 and 20 total, but there is no maximum number. It is important to note that if the partners do not have experience with each other, the identification of behavioral guidelines will be limited to and by each party's personal experience with others. In such cases, specific behavioral guidelines will focus on suggested "dos" and "don'ts" and then later on "stop/start/continue" suggestions.

When conducted effectively, this process provides the opportunity for both partners to address the issues and behaviors in the relationship that are very often considered "undiscussable." It gives both parties the opportunity to listen actively to the other's concerns, explore meaning, and ultimately commit, or not, to the other's stated or modified requests.

This process is one of the first key tests of the commitment to honesty that both partners are making in the PPA. It should be used to lay the groundwork for the thoughtful and honest communication that both parties will be employing as they work together as partners in the newly defined agreement.

## EXAMPLE:

Store manager requests of the DM:

### STOP:

> ➤ *Coming into the store and, without the involvement of the Manager on Duty, directing associates as to actions that need to be taken.*

> ➤ *Bringing large groups from the corporate or regional office into the store for a visit regarding a specific topic without giving advance notice so that schedules can be appropriately planned.*

> ➤ *Dictating to me how to run my store and then holding me accountable when your directions don't produce results.*

### START:

> ➤ *Spending a portion of each visit to the store engaging in dialogue with associates about store and company issues of relevance to them.*

> ➤ *Thanking department managers for a job well done when you notice that their department has met their numbers for the month.*

> ➤ *Brainstorming with me and my managers on difficult performance dilemmas.*

### CONTINUE:

> ➤ *Providing more coaching than directives*

> ➢ *Keeping me abreast of corporate initiatives that are likely to be of concern to me.*

> ➢ *Facilitating access to helpful resources within the corporation to help me address areas of opportunity in my store.*

DM requests of the store manager:

## STOP:

> ➢ *Raising sensitive or controversial issues with Corporate Store Support without keeping me informed.*

> ➢ *Taking formal disciplinary action with department managers without consulting HR and advising me in advance.*

> ➢ *Blaming and making excuses for your team.*

## START:

> ➢ *Keeping me abreast of development efforts with your department managers.*

> ➢ *Preparing in advance a list of strategic and organizational development issues and initiatives for discussion during my store visits.*

## CONTINUE:

> ➢ *Keeping me apprised of significant team performance concerns in the store that I need to be aware of so that there are few surprises.*

> ➢ *Developing managers to perform at or above target for their individual departments.*

> ➢ *Your excellent communication with all the associates in your store regarding the periodic performance of your store, your expectations of their individual and collective performance, the vision and goals for the company and the company's results.*

## 8. ACCOUNTABILITY AND CONSEQUENCES

As we have explored in detail, the PPA creates the framework for empowerment and a platform for accountability. Having done that in very specific detail, what's likely to happen if there are no periodic assessments and accountings of performance or discussion around the ramifications of either performing, or not performing, according to the defined expectations? Most likely, not very much. Remember:

**Accountability without consequences is wishful thinking.**

It is critical in a stewardship for the store manager to own his or her performance, problems, behavior, results and the related consequences inherent in each. Key drivers toward that true level of ownership and partnership include: (1) reporting-partner initiated assessments and accounting of performance in relation to agreed responsibilities and expectations, and (2) a thorough understanding of the consequences, both positive and negative, resulting from both partners' behavior and performance.

Regarding the first requirement, we suggest that both partners agree on what measurements are indicated and what information is necessary for the reporting partner (e.g. store manager) to sufficiently account for his or her performance. Such evaluations might include periodic inspections of store conditions initiated by the reporting partner, or store manager, third party store team profiling and interviewing, and periodic two-way performance reviews of and by both partners. Reports might include standard sales, profit and operating reports as well as special reports as needed and called for.

Regarding the second requirement, positive consequences would include monetary rewards such as bonuses or salary increases. They might also include other forms of recognition such as increased responsibility and/or authority in decision-making and, ultimately, the advancement to higher-level positions in the company.

The potential negative consequences range from specific corrective action, including adjustments of responsibility and authority levels, to removal from position and repositioning to another role in the organization, to termination of employment for not performing consistently with defined expectations.

More difficult to discern are the emotional reactions that may occur in response to the other partner's attitudes, behavior and actions. These, too, need to be honestly and openly explored up front and as they occur. This portion of the PPA process is not about developing a list of consequences that would be invoked as a result of the store manager's performance. Rather, it should be an in-depth conversation in which the partners explore their behavioral differences and the possible personal and business consequences they might trigger. This need not generate a written list of consequences - although it could. These could also be described in a summary paragraph of topics discussed. This conversation need not be construed as anything more than an exploration of natural consequences, both positive and negative, that stem from behavior and performance. In other words, the reporting partner is not being put on notice of unacceptable performance or being advised of any specific action that will or will not be taken under particular future circumstances.

Several questions can be posed for the dialogue session between the partners around consequences. Both parties need to listen carefully to their own reactions and to each other, inquiring about meaning, and balancing advocacy of their own views with inquiry into the other's views.

Some initial questions might include:

> *As a partner, what might be some potential positive/negative business and personal consequences related to the performance of this agreement?*

> *As a partner, how might you react in a situation where I acted or responded by doing x? Or, in situations where y happens, I typically react in this way... Or, if you were the managing/ reporting partner in a situation where z happens, what consequences do you think might be reasonable or justified under the circumstances?*

Remember, the desired outcome from this conversation around consequences is increased awareness and understanding. It is not about defining and recording any specific consequences that may or may not be invoked in hypothetical circumstances. Such specific consequences, if not required by policy, are determined on a case-by-case basis when particular situations arise.

The eight elements above make up the structure of the PPA between a DM and the store manager, although the same elements pertain to every PPA.

## ISN'T SOMEONE STILL "IN CHARGE" IN THIS PARTNERSHIP?

In most two-person business partnerships, one of them has a 51 percent say in any given matter. That's a reality of the business world, and it is important that we recognize it as a reality in the managing-reporting partner relationship. It is a reality of the structure of any organization and is, accordingly, reflected in the process and content of the partnership agreement.

So while the partnering process is designed to stimulate robust dialogue and spirited discussions, when it comes to a final decision on a particular issue, the manager reserves the right to exercise that 51 percent authority as a "managing partner." As Block so thoughtfully put it:

> *Partnership does not mean that you will always get what you want. It means that you may lose your argument from time to time but you will never lose your voice.*

At the end of the process, though, each party must genuinely feel, without hesitation, that at least 75 percent of himself or herself truly agrees that the terms and conditions of the agreement are reasonable, achievable and acceptable. When this level of 75 percent consensus is reached, both parties have arrived at "yes," and each becomes, through their respective acceptance, 100 percent accountable for providing the agreed upon support, performance and results. They both need to stay in the conversation with each other until they have reached that level of agreement, where both parties can honestly say that they feel at least 75 percent in accord with the terms and conditions.

When the Partnership Agreement process is complete, both partners should be clear about what is expected of them. If the agreement has been established and ratified by a hard earned and earnest "yes" from both parties, then the partnership is initiated and performance accountability is born. As two partners function in an adult relationship, there is no more need for parental, structural oversight or handholding. There also will be no childlike whining, complaining or finger pointing. The defensive avoidance of responsibility will be greatly minimized.

To arrive at such a place, there must be honesty and openness on the part of both parties. Both parties need to be committed to *collaborative* approaches that require the production of valid, actionable information as the basis for free, informed choice. They need to also be committed to *discussing the undiscussable*, to openly expressing all thoughts and concerns in order to create a relationship built on an honest foundation.

So as you can see, being "empowered" doesn't simply mean being knowledgeable and experienced. Nor does it mean having training or the tools needed to perform a job. From our perspective, to be empowered means to be fully and willingly engaged as a responsible partner with a voice and with all the decision-making rights and resources necessary to fulfill the delegated stewardship.

Baseline empowerment requires 'partnering' toward the acceptance of a clear stewardship, with all its elements as set forth above in the PPA. Further, such partnering requires that both parties involved be wholeheartedly engaged in the pursuit of a sufficient level of consensus through collaboration and creative negotiation designed to get to "yes." Beyond that, both partners must continue to review and revise their agreement periodically and support each other as needed and agreed on an ongoing basis.

The above ideal, of course, doesn't always work out. There might be irresolvable ideological differences between the partners concerning, for example, the nature of "partnership" or "commitment" and the requirements of "risk" and "sacrifice" inherent in such commitment. There might also be irresolvable differences regarding the content, requirements and limitations associated with the various elements of the agreement itself. Or, there might be a fundamental lack of sufficient maturity or ego strength in either or both partners, or deeper defenses and dynamics at play between the two that make adult interaction and negotiation too difficult. (Note: For a more in depth treatment of such defenses and dynamics, see the Author's book, *Working Beneath the Surface* (1996), Executive Excellence Publishing, Chapters 2-4.)

Such difficulties can be avoided to a degree through what is known in Action Science as "left-hand column (LHC) work." This work, developed by Chris Argyris, essentially requires those parties involved in a problem-solving conversation to check out questions or concerns they might have regarding another's meanings, intentions, actions, behavior or motivations. This needs to be done during the course of the conversation, typically by playing back statements made and/or asking questions that would reveal what the person "means" or "feels," or where the other is "at" or is "coming from."

If we were to write out the actual conversation between the parties involved in a right-hand column, then the unspoken thoughts or questions in the minds of those parties as they occur during the course of the conversation would be placed in the left-hand column. These LHC thoughts typically occur in reaction to something the other has said, or not said, or the way it was said, or not said. They usually take the form of an implicit accusation or question of curiosity or concern.

Left-hand column work is an indispensable skill not only in dealing with thorny partnership concerns, but also in analyzing and designing past and future accountability and learning conversations. We will revisit LHC work in Chapter 5 when we present a process for conversational design and a developmental approach to store visits.

As we look back on our own difficult conversations with others, we will no doubt find numerous instances of unspoken concerns and questions that were never checked out, but lingered in our LHC in the form of a conclusion, or fact. These LHC contents can be decisive in determining how we act or react toward others. Ultimately, they can accumulate and become increasingly malignant over time until they destroy the relationship or partnership.

There are no guarantees that any approach will work to establish or save a partnership. The most either a managing or reporting partner can do is attempt to work through the process, issues and concerns as maturely as possible.

Given the above and other possible pitfalls, it becomes evident that the managing partner might need to exercise his prerogative to make a final offer, or one or both of the individuals might need to withdraw and move in a different direction. It has been said that in creative negotiations "no deal" must always be an option. This option should be exercised as a last resort, however, after every effort has been made to get to a genuine "yes."

Over time, the partnership agreement process between existing partners will take less time and the formal agreement itself will become ancillary to the communicated and confirmed understanding of the agreement. This is because the partnership will have sufficiently evolved and the parties sufficiently matured in their communications and experience together. Still, ongoing 'partnering conversations' are always necessary as roles, responsibilities and expectations change, and as experience and performance warrant the appropriate adjustment of decision rights and operating guidelines to better balance the need for release and control.

## ACCOUNTABILITY AND THE MANAGEMENT OF RESULTS

We have been fascinated by how sophisticated and subtle some store managers and associates can be at evading accountability, and how selectively impotent some VPs and DMs are, at times, at doing anything about it. It's not that they don't see what is happening. They do. And it's not that they can't do anything about it. They can. They just *won't* do anything about it. So they just keep evading accountability, all the while asserting that they're "holding their people accountable," when what they're really doing is enduring non-performance until it becomes necessary to remove the store manager. When that happens, the cycle of non-performance starts all over again with the new replacement. This makes the breakdown of accountability primarily a character problem with both partners, where one or both individuals lack the required desire, commitment or emotional resources needed to honor the agreement in full. Let's take a deeper look.

As we said previously, accountability is derived from true empowerment. Performance accountability is ownership by free, informed choice. We as leaders *cannot* "hold people accountable" for their performance. This is one of the most widespread misconceptions in business today, and it's related to an even more grandiose belief that a manager or leader actually has the power to get his subordinates to "change" or do their jobs right. We cannot force or demand accountability or performance.

Rather, we can *enable* high-performance and *foster* accountability by collaborating toward a joint understanding of the terms and conditions of the partnership and the person's stewardship. This partnership understanding, derived through the Performance Partnership Agreement process, constitutes the baseline understanding.

What remains after establishing accountability *through* empowerment is: (1) resource deployment or allocation, as needed and agreed; (2) managing for results through periodic accountability conversations, as opposed to managing activities through direction, directives and follow-up; and (3) upgrading the team as needed in consequence of performance and results, or letting the consequences do their job. Of these three tasks of management, our concern here will focus on numbers two and three.

Accountability conversations are one of three ongoing and essential developmental conversations that field executives need to have with their reporting partners, the other two being partnering conversations and learning conversations. All three developmental conversations are presented in some depth in Chapter 5 in connection with a suggested, revised developmental store visit process.

The quest for empowerment, as we learned above, requires us to explore with our reporting partners our respective visions of the stewardship at hand, and then to collaborate and negotiate creatively to reach a sufficient consensus that will establish true engagement and ownership, or accountability, by choice. Such exploration is achieved through the crucial "partnering conversations" implied in the process presented earlier.

In *managing for results*, we need to explore the results of our performance in relation to the PPA, as well as the root cause of significant variances and possible corrective courses of action. We need to provide constructive feedback on an ongoing basis (without providing specific remedies or directives), explore changes that need to be made, and together formulate strategies for making them.

Finally, we need to explore the possible positive and negative consequences to the business and to each of us personally and collectively if the needed changes are made, or not made. Ultimately, if needed changes are not made and results become intolerable, both partners will understand why and what actions must be taken as part of the ongoing requirement for upgrading the team.

Just as partnering conversations can be difficult when the parties reach an impasse, so accountability conversations become difficult when either party fails to deliver promised support or results. These can be one of those "Advil conversations," as one executive aptly put it. Consider the following exchange between a managing partner (MP) and a reporting partner (RP):

*MP*: *"How'd we do in sales (or expenses) this period?"*

*RP*: *"Not well. I missed plan by 27%."*

*MP*: *"Are you able to account for the drop?"*

*RP*: *"We've looked at it pretty hard and, based on our root-cause analysis, found that it was caused by..."*

*MP*: *"When can you expect to make up for this drop and get back on track?"*

*RP*: *"I'm looking at 12 weeks."*

**MP**: *"That won't work. We've got to see a recovery of the loss in 45 days to meet plan. You and your team need to find a way to make this happen. Can you use me as a resource in some way?"*

**RP**: *"I think it would be helpful if you would participate in one or two of our think tank meetings. We could use another perspective to brainstorm with us."*

**MP**: *"Fine, let me know when and where and I'll be there. Meanwhile, I think we need to talk about the fact that this is the third time in 6 months that we've been in this predicament. I'm very concerned. What's similar and what's different among the three instances and what are your take-aways? I mean, what are your learnings about yourself as a leader and your team?"*

**RP**: *"What I'm seeing is... and what I'm learning about me is... and about my team is..."*

**MP**: *"What do these learnings suggest to you in terms of your own developmental needs and what you might need to do to further upgrade your team?"*

**RP**: *"They suggest, I believe, that..."*

**MP**: *"Here's what I'm seeing... I'm basing these thoughts on...To me this suggests that maybe...Am I missing anything in my thinking? What's your reaction?"*

**(RP and MP exchange thoughts.)**

**MP**: *"So, given the history of performance in your store, let's talk for a moment about what happens, from your perspective, if you and your team aren't able to deliver these results. Where does that leave us and what do you think would be a reasonable outcome based on our PPA?"*

If we could measure discomfort in degrees of Fahrenheit, the above conversation would be hot indeed! Development doesn't come easily, however, and is often facilitated by the 'heat' of performance and learning anxiety. Such anxiety is rooted in our willingness to change in order to improve performance and avoid the consequences of failing to do so.

Too often, field executives fail to facilitate development by first failing to empower their direct reports, then by failing to have the essential accountability conversations, and finally by failing to allow the agreed consequences of non-performance to do their job. This, of course, is the same as failing to upgrade their team. Again, accountability without consequences is wishful thinking. Consequences are essential to development and to performance. The failure to manage for results is not merely a style preference. It's a character failure rooted in a defensive orientation to action.

## LEARNING THROUGH REFLECTIVE COLLABORATION

Learning is the third fundamental of the Leadership Factor. The future of any competitive organization today depends on how effectively that organization can learn from its successes and its failures.

In part because the IDC approach to retail field management creates an anti-learning environment, we continue to do the same things over and over again and expect different results. Further, as our research shows, even the so-called "new" things we're trying are, in essence, the same old things. It's like we are trapped in a box and the directions for getting out of the box are written on the outside.

Learning is related to action and results, and is the outcome of working with others in a collaborative effort to research and design more effective solutions to our high-leverage process and execution problems. Learning is commonly viewed much more narrowly as being synonymous with "training." Let's look at how they differ.

Training involves imparting procedural or technical information necessary to perform a particular task. As leaders, we train others by teaching, showing and modeling a particular skill to accomplish a task.

Facilitating learning involves engaging people in a process that requires them to "manage their ignorance" to see the shortcomings or limitations of their orientation, thinking and approach and then to research, design, test, and revise new approaches for better results.

When we have been taught or shown how to perform a particular task and we can perform that task on our own, we have been trained. When we come to see our own ignorance, appreciate other viewpoints, understand how our own actions, skilled or otherwise, are resulting in unwanted results, and then collaboratively participate in creating alternative approaches that produce desired results, we are *learning*.

## REACTIVE VS. REFLECTIVE LEARNING AND PROBLEM SOLVING

Learning, in the context of actions and outcomes, is facilitated through the various approaches we take to solving performance problems. In this context there are typically two learning and/or problem-solving responses to an error or failure to perform:

o   *Reactive, Experience-Based Learning and Problem Solving*

o   *Reflective, Research and Design-Based Learning and Problem Solving*

## REACTIVE LEARNING AND PROBLEM SOLVING

*Reactive learning and problem solving* addresses problems out of past experience. It is best used when we engage in or involve others in basic, unreflective trial and error problem solving intended to "fix" low-leverage "presenting" and "process" level problems.

This form of learning is often used in the IDC approach to store visits and can easily be recognized by the questions asked to the store manager such as: "What could (or will) you do to fix this problem?" or "What could (or will) you do differently?" The store manager responds, out of his experience and with little to no reflection, with actions that he will take to correct the problem. The VP or DM agrees or provides, out of his own experience, a different experience-based solution.

## REFLECTIVE LEARNING AND PROBLEM SOLVING

*Reflective learning and problem solving* collaboratively addresses complex, non-routine and recurring "process," "team," and "management" performance problems through action research, design and experimentation.

To more clearly understand the difference between *reactive and reflective learning and problem solving*, consider this contrast:

➢   *With reactive learning and problem solving we act out of our experience, as if functioning on "auto pilot." This is appropriate when addressing "low-leverage" problems - simple, routine, non-recurring "presenting" and "process" level store problems that are insignificant, non-recurring or require immediate attention. When reactive learning is employed in dealing with complex, recurring, interactive performance problems, the problems recur and anti-learning results, as indicated in Chapter 1.*

➢ *With reflective learning and problem solving we collaboratively focus on:*

1. *Correctly defining the problem.*

2. *Assessing current or previous action taken and identifying the gap between intended and actual action and results.*

3. *Exploring and revising the underlying causes to action as needed (our facts, goals, intentions, desires, beliefs and assumptions. In other words, "where we're coming from" in taking action.)*

4. *Designing and testing new and improved solutions.*

*Reflective learning and problem solving is required when addressing high-leverage process and performance problems. Further, the research is clear that deep, lasting change resulting in consistent performance and effective execution requires reflective learning and problem solving.*

So what are high-leverage performance problems? As noted above, they are usually "team" and "management" level performance problems (and certain "process" level problems), which tend to possess one or more of the following characteristics:

➢ *Complex in nature, without single answers or simple resolution*

➢ *Interactive, with multiple variables at play or individuals involved*

➢ *Resistant to resolution – recurring in nature*

➢ *Potentially embarrassing or personally threatening*

Learning, then, is the action-based outcome of *creative collaboration* in which people are: (1) engaged to look critically at the limitations of their historical thinking and approaches to problem solving, and then (2) research, design and test new approaches that have a substantially higher probability of solving the problem or achieving the desired results.

To appreciate more how this reflective, collaborative approach to learning works, it might be helpful to finally consider the nature and practice of collaboration and then translate the idea of such learning to a coaching process that we teach and use with our clients.

## COLLABORATION

To collaborate means to work *with* others toward the achievement of a mutually determined solution of a high-leverage performance problem. It is an inclusive process, in which the participants work together to manage their ignorance and co-create a better solution than they most likely ever could have created on their own.

Collaboration requires mutual respect and a commitment to development and the best ideas and solutions, as opposed to winning or being right. Collaboration can be effectively used to identify problems, stimulate ideas, challenge thinking and assumptions, explore possibilities, design potential strategies, and plan options for resolution and execution. Used properly in a culture that embraces development and learning, it is a powerful tool.

True collaboration requires the discovery and exploration of each other's thinking. This is most effectively accomplished through open-ended questions focused on: w*hat?* h*ow?* w*hy?* But it doesn't stop there. Beyond such probing there is the need to work through the problem to its resolution. One of the best approaches for doing this is what is called *balancing advocacy and inquiry.*

## BALANCING ADVOCACY AND INQUIRY

Balancing advocacy and inquiry is an approach that was initially designed by Chris Argyris and is referenced by a variety of management authors, including Peter Senge in his revolutionary work on the subject of organizational learning in *The Fifth Discipline.* One of the reasons that the process is so powerful is that it focuses on the ideas, premises, or conclusions being presented, rather than people or personalities, and is blind to status and rank. The goal is to facilitate learning and more effective action and decision-making through balanced reasoning and the production of valid information.

To better appreciate this learning tool, we need to understand the idea it's based on. We're referring here to Argyris' "ladder of inference." The idea of the ladder of inference is fundamental to all three tools of Action Science presented in this book, including left-hand column work, *reflective learning and problem solving* (which Argyris terms "double-loop learning"), and balancing advocacy and inquiry. All three of these tools are invaluable in applying the Leadership Factor to "management" level problems to achieve great store performance.

## THE LADDER OF INFERENCE

The ladder of inference (see Figure 4 below) teaches us that we act on the basis of self-generating beliefs which remain largely untested. These beliefs, which we erroneously equate with truth, make us selectively attentive and determine in large measure what we focus on in any given situation. They also tend to shape the meanings, assumptions and conclusions we attach to certain facts, making them self-reinforcing. Such a self-reinforcing mechanism tends to attach, in turn, to those beliefs that serve our self-interests. If so, it would likely be defensively motivated, perhaps by our needs for safety, security and esteem.

# FIGURE 4:
## LADDER OF INFERENCE

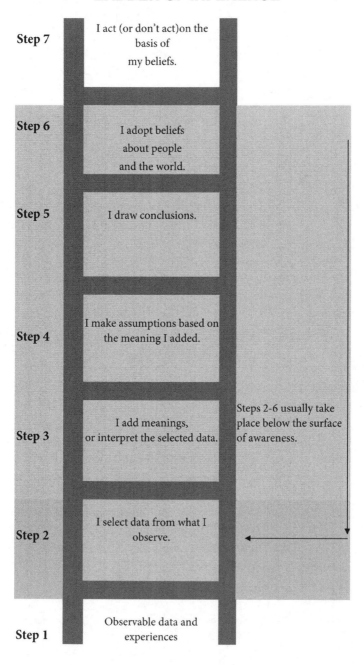

Step 7 — I act (or don't act)on the basis of my beliefs.

Step 6 — I adopt beliefs about people and the world.

Step 5 — I draw conclusions.

Step 4 — I make assumptions based on the meaning I added.

Step 3 — I add meanings, or interpret the selected data.

Steps 2-6 usually take place below the surface of awareness.

Step 2 — I select data from what I observe.

Step 1 — Observable data and experiences

What's relevant here is the idea that this ladder of inference is a metaphor for the way we reach (or "jump to") conclusions and how such conclusions are usually unconsciously contaminated by misguided, self-reinforcing beliefs. Here's how it works: a DM walks in a store and is struck by the long lines at the checkout registers. He immediately reacts negatively and directs the store manager to call more cashiers to the front.

What happened here that triggered this action? First, this DM entered the store with certain beliefs about the store manager and certain assumptions about what he might find. These beliefs and assumptions conditioned and directed his focus. All he saw was long lines (observed and selected data). From here he defensively, unconsciously, and instantaneously climbs his ladder of inference to reinforce his belief that the store manager was not responding to the customer. "The long lines mean that the customer is being ignored (added meaning)." "This has been going on like this for quite a while and no one has been called to the front to assist (assumptions)." "Clearly the store manager doesn't care about customer service (belief reinforcing conclusion)." "Not only is this a violation of brand standards, it reflects poorly on me (setting the DM up to lose)." "I need to fix this situation now (takes unilateral control of the store)."

Since we all jump to conclusions continually, we need a way to climb down our ladders of inference with others to manage our ignorance. In doing so, we can focus on the right problems in the right way, make the best decisions possible through valid information, and not make matters worse by intervening inappropriately.

In our example above, the DM might have better served the store, the customer, and the store manager by finding the store manager and doing the LHC work needed to check out his assumptions and conclusions first. If the situation was truly critical, stepping in first to give direction would certainly be appropriate. Even so, the LHC work would need to be done. Then, if there was indeed a performance problem, follow-up partnering, accountability and *reflective learning* conversations would be called for.

With this background understanding of the "ladder of inference," we can perhaps better appreciate how collaboration in general, and the skill of balancing advocacy and inquiry in particular, is a mutual pursuit of valid information and understanding. It doesn't consist of one person asking all the questions, as an inquisitor, with the other person on the defensive, feeling as though he must come up with all the right answers or solutions.

Balancing advocacy and inquiry is a skill that requires every person involved in the collaboration to offer opinions, conclusions, or ideas, present their facts and reasoning, and invite others to critically explore or challenge both through probative inquiry. On the one hand, you are advocating a position, inviting critical inquiry and responding with more information or further questions.

On the other hand, you are listening critically to the ideas, challenges, and conclusions offered or advocated by others, and inquiring, with a genuine curiosity and an open mind, to learn something about the perspective, experiences, and opinions of the other person. The effective balance of advocacy and inquiry means that you are playing two different roles, with equal emphasis in a process of discovery and continuous learning. Such a process requires the partner-collaborators to walk each other either up or down their respective ladders of inference as needed.

The balance is not easy to achieve. We all have predispositions. People who study law, for example, are taught to perfect the skill of advocacy, even when asking questions. You can imagine the difficulty a skilled litigator might have if suddenly tasked with being truly open minded, without any agenda, especially in a situation where the attorney has an established opinion on the matter. Gender might also play a role: men are culturally expected to be much more advocacy-oriented, while, women are thought to be less opinionated and more inquisitive.

Prior programming in the business world also inhibits our ability to balance advocacy and inquiry, as does our orientation to action. Most senior managers have learned over the course of their careers to refine their ability to synthesize ideas, formulate conclusions and solve problems. They have also perfected the skill of advocating their views, which, by definition, might leave them less adept at effective inquiry. While these problem-solving skills may serve them well when dealing with routine, low-leverage problems, more complex problems require a higher level of thinking and collaboration with other knowledgeable colleagues to arrive at viable, sustainable solutions.

If a person is functioning out of a defensive orientation to action, balancing advocacy and inquiry will be very difficult. As we will learn in the next chapter, this particular orientation to action is built on the social virtues of winning and not losing and saving face. These types of values incline us to act in ways that make the balancing of advocacy and inquiry difficult and very unlikely at best.

One way of approaching advocacy and inquiry could look like this. You state your opinion about the issue that is up for discussion. You lay out your reasoning and the assumptions you are making that lead you to your view. Then you encourage others to challenge it. For example, "Here is my view . . . here are the facts as I understand them . . . here is my reasoning . . . and here is how I arrived at my conclusions . . . How does this sound to you? What makes sense and what doesn't? What might I be missing? Are my assumptions valid? Do you see any ways I can improve upon the approach I'm considering?"

There are strong and weak forms of both inquiry and advocacy. Strong inquiry means asking tough questions designed to validate facts, explore motives and intentions, and penetrate defensive reasoning or resistance. Examples of strong inquiry might be: "How do you square your facts with... (contradicting or different facts)?" "What do you stand to gain by taking this course of action?" "How does your reasoning get you from (A) to (B)?" "What are you assuming here and why?"

Weak inquiry often takes the form of soft questions, designed not to embarrass the other person or to support a particular position being advocated. For example, "Wouldn't you agree that...?" "You're really saying... right?"

Strong advocacy, as illustrated three paragraphs earlier, makes a claim (even an impassioned claim!) and then backs it up by revealing the assumptions, meanings, and facts used to reach the conclusion, as well as the bias of the advocate's personal beliefs that might have determined the focus of his thinking.

Weak advocacy is bullying and intimidating advocacy. "This is the way I see it... (and you'd have to be a fool or blind not to see it my way)." Or, "As everybody knows (or the facts clearly show)..." Combining both weak advocacy and weak inquiry might look like this: "Clearly, this is the way we need to approach this, right?" Who hasn't experienced this bad joke?

Balancing advocacy and inquiry can hurt people's egos by attacking their coveted opinions, which is one reason why it is so difficult to master. But the payoff comes in the more creative and insightful realizations and the stronger courses of action that occur when people combine their perspectives and respectfully but honestly confront their own and others' blind spots and defensive reasoning.

In the Appendix to this Chapter, titled "Protocols for Balancing Advocacy and Inquiry," we have borrowed from Senge's *Fifth Discipline Fieldbook* (1994) to illustrate some conversational protocols and examples of this approach, providing some ways of effectively exposing your thinking processes, testing your conclusions and assumptions, and encouraging others to join you in a collaborative process to do the same.

## A COACHING METHODOLOGY FOR FACILITATING REFLECTIVE LEARNING

In a partnership that values collaboration, coaching on the part of a designated "peer coach" or the managing partner is a valuable tool to further the development of the reporting partner. What follows is a coaching methodology that is designed to facilitate *reflective learning* through mutual discovery, exploration, analysis, collaboration and open testing. (This is presented in contrast to a more typical coaching approach by retail field executives, which would include providing answers, tips, ideas, or sharing "best practices" from other stores. While executives feel they are being helpful by sharing all this good information, it's not coaching, at least by our definition, and very little learning is going on.)

## FACILITATED PROBLEM SOLVING COACHING PROCESS:

*1. Define the level and nature of the problem.*

*Consider together the following:*

➢ *What is the presenting problem?*

➢ *Is it a recurring problem or a new problem?*

➢ *Is it a process problem?*

➢ *Is it a team performance problem?*

➢ *Is it a management performance problem?*

➢ *Is the issue a deficiency in skills?*

➢ *Is the problem the result of an attitude?*

*2. Determine what actions have been (were) taken to address the problem.*

*Use illustrative questions such as:*

➢ *How have you been addressing this problem?*

> ➤ *What various approaches have you used in an attempt to solve this problem?*

3. *Determine the outcomes of action taken.*

   *Again, use illustrative questions such as:*

   > ➤ *What happened? How do you know?*

   > ➤ *Why do you think this outcome occurred?*

   > ➤ *How did you arrive at that conclusion?*

4. *Determine where the person is coming from in taking future action. To do so, explore and identify the person's underlying goals, intentions, motives, beliefs, assumptions, and criteria for success in moving forward.*

*Some illustrative questions to get at these:*

> ➤ *What do you want/need to accomplish? Why is that important?*

> ➤ *Why do you think this problem is so hard to solve? What don't you know that might help this problem come into greater focus?*

> ➤ *What do you think is getting in the way of your success? What don't you know that might help you better understand the resistance to change you're experiencing?*

> ➤ *How did you arrive at these conclusions?*

> ➤ *How might your beliefs in this case influence your approach?*

> ➤ *How could you determine whether your beliefs are valid or invalid?*

> ➤ *What would success look like? What are the success criteria you will use to determine the best approach in this situation?*

> ➤ So, what are your intentions moving forward? Is this about taking control or development?

> ➤ Then what is it about? What else?

5. *Balance advocacy and inquiry to collaborate on actions to be taken, including necessary conversations to test conclusions and explore solutions.*

*Some illustrative questions:*

> ➤ Given your goals and intentions, how could you approach this problem differently in order to get a consistently better outcome?

> ➤ What's your reasoning with that approach?

> ➤ What does it accomplish?

> ➤ How so?

> ➤ What about. . . (offer an idea or suggestion)?

> ➤ Here's my thinking. . . (walk down your ladder of inference).

> ➤ What do you think about that potential approach?

> ➤ Which approach would best satisfy your stated goals and criteria for success? How so?

> ➤ How could you test your conclusions to determine whether or not they are valid? What's your thinking here?

> ➤ What about. . . (offer more thoughts or ideas).

> ➤ Here's my thinking. . . (share your reasoning).

> ➤ What are your thoughts?

6. *Play out options and test against success criteria. Collaborate to come to closure on the conversational design of the solution.*

*Some illustrative questions:*

> *What would this approach look like in terms of action and behavior? (Walk through the actions)*

> *How might this conversation play out? (Role play, 'you say/the other says.' Explore LHC thoughts by both parties.)*

> *What's the likelihood of success given how this played out? How so?*

> *Here are my thoughts/concerns. . .*

> *Here is my thinking. . .*

> *I suggest. . . Here's why. . .*

> *What if you tried this. . .?*

> *What do you think? Why?*

7. *If possible and feasible, observe the person in action, note any performance gaps, and debrief afterward to discuss learnings and outcomes and to collaborate on refinements as needed.*

*Some illustrative questions:*

> *What did you experience?*

> *What were you trying to accomplish? Is that what you wanted?*

> *Here's what I observed. . . (be specific with supporting facts).*

> *What were the outcomes from your point of view?*

> *Why the gap(s)?*

> ➢   *What could you do to close the gaps?*

> ➢   *What would that look like?*

> ➢   *How about. . . (offer suggestions or thoughts).*

> ➢   *I'm wondering how the outcome might change for the better if you were to do . . . instead of . . . Here's why...*

> ➢   *What do you think? Why is that?*

## THE ENERGY OF SUSTAINED ENGAGEMENT

Empowerment and learning as envisioned in this chapter result in the development of others' talents into strengths and the birth of performance accountability. As the three fundamentals are incorporated in leadership action, they produce what we refer to as the "energy of sustained engagement," an energy that changes to internal commitment with the experience of sustained success in achieving objectives and solving complex problems.

It's not uncommon for individuals and store teams to experience what we refer to as the "energy of possibility" when changes regarded as positive are made through external interventions, when assistance is given by others in a non-threatening way, or attention and recognition for short term improvement is received from management. This *energy of possibility* is often short lived, however, if true development doesn't occur, promised change does not materialize, or results either do not occur or are not sufficiently sustained.

The 'energy of sustained engagement,' however, is result of the Leadership Factor – the dynamic interplay of empowerment, performance accountability, and *reflective learning*. This Leadership Factor is, we repeat, indispensable to "world class" performance in organizations and therefore to great store performance.

## RECAPITULATION

In this chapter we hope you've come to appreciate that the first dilemma of recurring problems in our stores builds on the second dilemma of inconsistent performance and results and requires a very different vision of the leadership task.

We learned in the first chapter that the prevailing, control-based approach to retail field management isn't working in pursuit of great store performance. The undesirable results it produces present seasoned field executives with three vexing dilemmas. The solution to the first two dilemmas lies in the need for field executives to radically revise their roles and focus on the store manager's ability and willingness to build and upgrade his store team.

This requires field executives and store managers to understand and apply the three fundamentals of high performance – *empowerment, accountability,* and *learning* - which come together dynamically as the essential Leadership Factor to sustained store improvement.

## THE MISSING LEADERSHIP FACTOR: REVISITED

Why is the Leadership Factor missing in all the existing approaches to retail field management researched to date?

Perhaps because the executives and managers in position are misplaced in terms of their talents, strengths and interests. This explanation, of course, fails to account for those cases where the Leadership Factor is absent and the leader is engaged, talented, and qualified according to company standards.

Another possible explanation is executive burnout, but this too fails to explain the absence of developmental leadership by those still engaged in their work.

Still another explanation might be ignorance: the leader in the field is simply uninformed or misinformed. This explanation does not account for the fact that some executives and store managers exposed to the three fundamentals through both action-based learning and coaching sessions do not continue to develop their people, even though they understand the importance of the three fundamentals, are personally qualified to facilitate the development of their direct reports, and are energized by the possibilities of doing so.

Then there is the explanation that VPs, DMs and store managers are "good" at what they do, get good enough results, and don't see or feel the need to change. This explanation apparently has teeth. A lot of field executives promoted to their current positions have done well for themselves and for their organizations by being positive, taking care of their people and taking firm control, producing a team of energized managers and associates that get good results.

Many of these "successful executives" who manage with the same counterproductive approach as their predecessors insist that their people are empowered, accountable and developed, although by stricter standards, they are not. These leaders, in our experience, fail to distinguish between the "energy of sustained engagement" and the "energy of possibility" presented earlier, or the attitudes of "commitment" and either "genuine compliance" or "enrollment" as suggested by Senge in Chapter 1. They also confuse the associate who is truly motivated with one who is merely not un-motivated, or compliant. There's a big difference, as we know, but one that cannot be distinguished by someone who does not know the difference.

In all of this, the assertions of success are usually based on unfounded optimism or are supported, at most, by soft, anecdotal evidence and numbers that define success on either a short term basis or on a relative basis using period comparables (comps). This, as we pointed-out in the Introduction, is far from great or world class store performance as we envision it and falls far short of what is truly possible. We will delve into the problem with your 'good' performing stores in Chapter 5.

Finally, there is the explanation that there's just not enough time, that applying the Leadership Factor just takes too long. This explanation, which is really an unfounded excuse, was dealt with in depth in the last chapter and found to be wanting.

Where does this leave us? We think that practicing the Leadership Factor of development is consistently undermined by a seemingly irresolvable competing commitment rooted in a company-wide defensive orientation to action.

Essentially, it just isn't believed to be safe, regardless of assurances to the contrary, to take the time to develop direct reports as suggested in this chapter. This is because, as everyone *knows* but doesn't say publicly, senior management doesn't *really* value empowerment or learning and doesn't *really* want empowered, committed managers and associates. Management is, in the final analysis, driven by short-term numbers and the performance expectations of Wall Street analysts and shareholders.

Consequently, what senior management seems to really want is for the VPs, DMs and store managers to fix the stores and keep them fixed and operating according to dictated standards. Empowered and internally committed employees are a threat that needs to be avoided. In reality, *good* store performance is good enough, and the price for *greatness* is too high.

The absence of the Leadership Factor of development can be best explained by what we have referred to earlier as a "defensive orientation to action," which we will explore in the next chapter as we wrestle with the third and final dilemma to the problem of inconsistent performance: why we persist in doing what doesn't work. We will then expose the flawed advice to retail executives that seduces them into believing that they are responding effectively to the leadership mandate of change or development when they are not. In fact, we will assert that some of the more popular leadership development programs offered today are, if not merely insufficient, counterproductive.

## KEY INSIGHTS FROM CHAPTER 3:

➢ *Inconsistent results are a failure of execution. When a store is unable to consistently produce targeted results, it is not effectively executing.*

➢ *What's missing is the Leadership Factor of development comprised of three fundamentals of effective execution: Empowerment, Accountability and Learning.*

➢ *The Performance Partnership Agreement (PPA) creates the framework for both empowerment and accountability. It clarifies the stewardship that is being invested in the individual and is the basis for that individual to be accountable for their performance.*

➢ *We as leaders cannot "hold people accountable" for their performance. We enable or foster accountability by creating clarity around expectations in a collaborative process that defines the terms of the person's stewardship.*

➢ *Deep lasting change resulting in consistent performance and effective execution requires reflective learning and problem solving.*

# APPENDIX:

# PROTOCOLS FOR BALANCING ADVOCACY AND INQUIRY

In his book *The Fifth Discipline Fieldbook* (1994, Currency-Doubleday), Peter Senge and his colleagues offer specific protocols for balancing advocacy and inquiry. In this section, we will present these protocols, which can easily be customized to the retail environment.

Balancing advocacy and inquiry is one way for individuals, by themselves, to propose new ideas, weigh in on important issues and to begin changing the team from within. The purpose of the following conversational recipes is to help people learn the skills of balancing advocacy and inquiry. Use them whenever a conversation offers you an opportunity to facilitate or participate in learning or contribute to problem-solving or decision-making in the stores or organization.

## PROTOCOLS FOR *ADVOCACY*

### Make your thinking process visible:

| What to do | What to say |
|---|---|
| State your conclusions, and describe the data that led to them. | "Here's what I think, and here's how I got there." |
| Explain your assumptions. | "I assumed that..." |
| Make your reasoning explicit. | "I came to this conclusion because..." |
| Explain the context of your point of view: Who will be affected by what you propose, how will they be affected, and why. | |
| Give examples of what you propose, even it they're hypothetical or metaphorical. | "To get a clear picture of what I'm talking about, imagine that you're the customer who will be affected..." |
| As you speak, try to picture the other people's perspectives on what you are saying. | |

# Publicly test your conclusions and assumptions:

| What to do | What to say |
|---|---|
| Encourage others to explore your model, your assumptions, and your data. | "What do you think about what I just said?" or "Do you see any flaws in my reasoning?" or "What can you add?" |
| Refrain from defensiveness when your ideas are questioned. If you're advocating something worthwhile, then it will only get stronger by being tested. | |
| Reveal where you are least clear in your thinking. Rather than making you vulnerable, it defuses the force of advocates who are opposed to you, and invites improvement. | "Here's one aspect which you might help me think through..." |
| Even when proposing, listen, stay open, and encourage others to provide different views. | "Do you see it differently?" |

## PROTOCOLS FOR *INQUIRY*

### Ask *others* to make their thinking processes visible:

| What to do | What to say |
| --- | --- |
| Respectfully explore others' inferences and find out what data they are operating from. | "What leads you to conclude that?" "What data do you have for that?" "What causes you to say that?" |
| Use non-aggressive language, particularly with people who are not familiar with these skills. Ask in a way which does not provoke defensiveness or "lead the witness." | Instead of "What do you mean?" or "What's your proof?" say, "Can you help me understand your thinking here?" or, "I'm not sure what that means, can you tell me more?" |
| Draw out their reasoning. Find out as much as you can about why they are saying what they're saying. | "What is the significance of that?" "How does this relate to your other concerns?" "Where does your reasoning go next?" |
| Explain your reasons for inquiring, and how your inquiry relates to your own concerns, hopes, and needs. | "I'm asking you about your assumptions here because…" |

## Compare your assumptions to theirs:

| What to do | What to say |
|---|---|
| Test what they say by asking for broader contexts, or for examples. | "How would your proposed course of action affect (or deal with)…?" "Is this similar to…?" "Can you describe a typical example…?" |
| Check your understanding of what they have said. | "Am I correct that you're saying…" |
| Listen for new understanding that may emerge. Don't concentrate on preparing to destroy the other person's argument or promote your own agenda. | |

# Protocols for facing a point of view with which you disagree:

| What to do | What to say |
|---|---|
| Again, inquire about what has led the person to that view. | "How did you arrive at this view?" "Are you taking into account data that I have not considered?" |
| Make sure you truly understand the view and can accurately and thoroughly re-state the view to the other person's satisfaction. Verify that you understand the view. | "If I understand you correctly, you're saying that…" "Do I have that correct? Do I understand correctly? |
| Explore, listen, and offer your own views in an open way. | "Have you considered…" |
| Listen for the larger meaning that may come out of honest, open sharing of alternative mental models. | |
| Raise your concerns and state what is leading you to have them. | "When you say such-and-such, I worry that it means…" "I have a hard time seeing that, because of this reasoning…" |

## C H A P T E R   4

# WHY WE PERSIST IN DOING WHAT DOESN'T WORK: DEFENSIVE ACTION, FLAWED ADVICE, AND COMPETING COMMITMENTS

*In this chapter:*

> *Why is it so difficult to act and behave according to our best plans and intentions?*

> *Why do our best efforts to change often leave us stuck in the same place?*

> *Why are we too often content to take action and make important decisions without valid information?*

> *Why don't new development programs produce promised results, and why do we keep taking advice that doesn't work?*

Why do we persist in doing what doesn't work?

The reason stems from an inherent resistance to change. The necessary changes we must make in our actions and behaviors to achieve great store performance – the empowerment, the learning - work against our deeply conditioned inclinations. They are unnatural to us, and because they differ so radically from our normal way of doing business, they seem very, very risky. Before we can realistically entertain the prospect of great store performance, we must understand the resistance to it that exists and why it exists. We need to examine what keeps us all stuck in our own *skilled incompetence* and makes necessary change feel unnatural and threatening. As a way of beginning, consider the following actual exchange between a consultant from our firm (**C**) and an executive with one of our clients (**E**), edited from the post-conversation transcript:

**E:** "We need to put development on hold for now."

**C:** "Why is that?"

**E:** "Because right now we've got to concentrate on execution in our stores. We've got to hit the numbers. We can't afford to distract our store managers and associates."

**C:** "But isn't that what these development efforts in the field are designed for and attempting to accomplish, better, more consistently effective execution?"

**E:** "Yes, but it's still a distraction."

**C:** "In what way?"

**E:** "Look, we need to free up the DMs to make sure the store managers are getting their teams to fix their stores to brand standards. They need to be in the trenches giving the associates the direction they need to get the tasks done to spec."

**C:** "So, you see the parallel coaching of RVPs and DMs to help store managers improve execution as a distraction?"

**E:** "At this point, yes. They don't have time to develop store managers. They've got to get in the stores and make sure the new programs and initiatives are getting executed."

**C:** "Stay with me for a moment. We both know that what you're suggesting takes the store managers' focus off their teams and reduces the VPs and DMs to compliance officers and de-facto store managers. You know that what you're doing is ultimately making store performance worse."

**E:** "Yes, I know, but that's the way it's always been, and I doubt if it will ever change."

**C:** "Not even in the face of compelling facts, reason and need?"

E: "Unfortunately, facts and reason have nothing to do with it. And we need to make the numbers and get these programs in place."

This executive knew first-hand that the stores were not executing to plan or brand. And he knew that the postponement of field coaching and development was only going to send mixed messages to the field leaders and make the problem worse. He also knew that this decision was motivated by his own defensive orientation to action, an inherent, fear-based resistance to change.

And so he persisted in doing what he knew wouldn't work. It was as if he and other executives were saying out of one side of their mouths, "We know that we can only achieve great store performance if our store managers and associates are truly empowered and accountable and are continually learning." And, at the same time, they were saying out of the other side of their mouths, "To hell with empowerment. To hell with accountability and learning. To hell with development and great store performance. We need to get in there and get the job done." It should be noted that this company was not in financial crisis or decline. It was performing well and ahead of plan. There was simply no need or reasonable justification for postponing development. Doing so would only cause considerable setback and harm.

At the heart of such irrational persistence was a deeply embedded set of values, beliefs, and assumptions that moved him, in spite of what he knew he wanted and agreed with, to act defensively. This he did to avoid the risk of disapproval and correction from his boss. This he did to "save face." This inclination to act defensively is known in Action Science as the "Model I" meta-theory of action. Others refer to it by different names. We have been referring to it in this book as simply the "Defensive Orientation to Action" (DOA).

## THE DEFENSIVE ORIENTATION TO ACTION (DOA)

This fundamental orientation to action is deeply ingrained in all of us through social conditioning from a very early age. It is a mind-set that includes the following core cultural values related to social success: (1) set goals and try to achieve them; (2) maximize winning and minimize losing (and loss), including the winning of esteem, approval, status, popularity, power, trust, loyalty, victory over others, material gain, recognition and other goods; (3) be positive and suppress negative emotion and criticism, particularly of leaders or authority figures; and (4) always appear (behave) rational(ly) by remaining calm, even-keeled and objective.

These core values serve our basic needs for survival, security, esteem and attachment. Since they are also necessary for the achievement of social success, why are they of concern?

For the answer, we need to look at another part of this hidden agenda. Not only do we all seek social success, but we're also motivated to avoid social failure. We are all naturally motivated to avoid embarrassment and the related loss of security, status, power, social acceptance and esteem. Such a goal is where we're coming from when we act defensively. The goal of success motivates us to employ strategies in our interactions with others that will advance our self-interests *and* protect us from failure and loss.

It is this goal that makes the core values defensive in nature. And it is often the second part of the goal-to avoid social failure- which contaminates the first part. In doing so, our interactive actions and behaviors in the workplace and elsewhere frequently become self-defeating and counterproductive.

Such a defensive orientation motivates us to employ action strategies to promote personal success and avoid the "negativity" of reality and the risk of losing face. They are as follows: (1) unilaterally control the environment to accomplish the goals *you* set; (2) persuade others to get buy-in to *your* requirements, expectations, plans or points of view; (3) own and control the tasks and methods *you* have determined are necessary to be performed through telling, directing, advising, or prescribing actions to be taken; (4) protect yourself and others; and (5) play nice, at least to others' faces.

These defensively oriented action strategies are reinforced by an unspoken set of *rules of control* deeply embedded in our Western culture and, consequently, in our institutional and corporate cultures. They are as follows:

1. *The authority figure is always right.*

2. *Do what you're told, no matter what.*

3. *Don't talk back.*

4. *Don't rock the boat.*

5. *Don't think, feel, or act in ways the authority figure would disapprove of.*

6. *Don't need, want, or value anything the authority figure thinks is inappropriate.*

7. *Don't learn, say, think, or do anything that might threaten the authority figure.*

8. *Don't screw up or make mistakes; if anything goes wrong, blame yourself or others, and refer to rule #1.*

What is most troubling is how easily and thoroughly we can all deceive ourselves into believing that we do not act on the basis of such rules of control in spite of all the confirmed evidence to the contrary. To better appreciate this orientation to action and the action strategies that define it, let's translate them into observable defensive actions and routines. Below are several we have observed:

- *Engage in defensive problem solving by: (1) immediately forming a conclusion regarding the nature of the problem and looking only for examples to confirm it; (2) not seeking evidence to disprove the conclusion; (3) being very resistant to change the conclusion, even when it is obviously wrong; (4) adopting overly simple strategies for solution if the problem is too complex; (5) adopting such solutions without challenging their underlying assumptions.*

- *Present only positive and supportive evidence to forward an agenda or proposal to get buy-in.*

- *Tell others what you think will make them feel good about themselves to exert greater control. This includes reducing their performance anxiety, discomfort, or hurt by either siding with them, letting them off the hook, or trying to make things better for them.*

- *Protect others from being hurt by withholding or softening information, creating rules to censure information and behavior, holding private meetings, etc.*

- *Defer to other people, particularly those in authority, and do not question their reasoning or actions.*

- *Advocate your position in order to win. Hold your own position in the face of disagreement. Evaluate others' thoughts and suggestions as being flawed on the sole basis of your differing opinion or experience and resist others' ideas on the basis of conflicting beliefs rather than valid information.*

- *Protect yourself. Save face by: agreeing to something you either don't understand or don't agree with, pleading ignorance or confusion, shifting blame, rationalizing, denying, waiting and seeing, suppressing feelings or intellectualizing.*

- *Own and control the task as its creator, owner and guardian of meaning and execution. Do this by "micro-managing" others.*

To further appreciate what it's like to operate from this particular orientation at a more personal level, consider the following sentence completions and apply them honestly to yourself:

"You know you are operating out of the DOA when...

- *You interact with direct reports from a "parent"script and with bosses, or authority figures, from a "child" script. Acting as a "parent", you value obedience, conformity. loyalty. compliance and good behavior and tend to exert control through reward, recognition, caring and intimidation to get what you want. Your behavior is characterized and experienced as being directive, condescending, patronizing, evaluative, judgmental and threatening.*

  *Acting as a "child", you value recognition, reward, trust, acceptance and fairness and strive to win the favor of the boss, follow the rules and do what you're told. Your behavior is characterized and experienced as being manipulative and defensive, playing the role of the "victim" when held accountable by others, particularly authority figures.*

- *your intention in engaging, questioning or intervening is to act on others to make, motivate or even help them to do what you want them to do*

- *you hesitate in asking tough accountability questions, or in waiting for the other person to answer*

- *you feel the need to rescue the other person's esteem and loyally – gallantly - come to their defense, or you act to make the other feel better, eliminate anxiety, preserve morale, or otherwise enable others' incompetence, laziness or irresponsibility by letting them off the hook with respect to their accountability or development*

- *you refuse to question your deeply held assumptions or beliefs*

- *you agree with something that you really disagree with in order to save face or avoid conflict or discomfort*

- *you provide calculated verbal recognition to improve morale or get (i.e. manipulate) others to work harder and smarter, to keep up the good work*

- *you avoid confrontation for fear of being seen as negative or not a team player*

- *you compromise your personal commitment to do what you need to do to succeed by waiting to see what the hierarchy will do or how they react to others*

- *you feel threatened by the autonomy, initiative or commitment of direct reports and feel the need to reel them in and keep them in line rather than explore their approach in the context of their development."*

Certainly no one does all of these things all the time. Still we do know, by direct observation of executives, managers and associates in action, that all of us act and behave in some of these ways some of the time and many, if not most, people do so very frequently.

The point is this: acting defensively severely compromises performance and accountability. Acting defensively is also natural to all of us. We are all socially and culturally conditioned to do so. Unfortunately, however, such a defensive orientation to action resists our commitment to "great" organizational and store performance and keeps us stuck in doing what we know doesn't work.

In addition to the actions and behaviors above, the DOA ultimately contaminates our various problem-solving approaches and thereby translates to the well-known direct and indirect control-based approaches to field management we have already discussed. These and other control-based management approaches are defensive routines that are management's ways of avoiding failure and the threat of loss by covering up non-performers and covering their own rear-ends too.

As we have analyzed these approaches with the VPs and DMs we have coached in the field, we have found that not only are they motivated defensively, but they are also built on certain fatal assumptions.

## FATAL ASSUMPTIONS

An assumption is fatal to its support of a conclusion if it is not based on valid information and sound reasoning. Here are some of the most common fatal assumptions about store managers used by field executives to justify their control-based hit and run approaches to field leadership:

## THE STORE MANAGER...

- *has the same sense of urgency and priority as I do.*

- *understands, accepts, and agrees with all the terms of the PPA.*

- *sees things the way I do.*

- *has based his/her approach on valid information.*

- *is internally committed to the vision and the work.*

- *truly owns his/her actions, behavior and results.*

- *is empowered to change his approach.*

- *understands the true nature of the problem.*

- *knows what to do and how to do it.*

- *knows how to effectively build and upgrade his/her team.*

- *would approach the problem the way it needs to be done.*

- *means what I mean in shared communication.*

- *wants to be a store manager and has the talents for the job and the strengths to do it well.*

As a field executive, your general, vague feedback and superficial directives won't help much if these assumptions aren't valid. And there's nothing in your approach that can verify the assumptions since, by definition, their validity is assumed.

These assumptions constitute the field executive's ignorance. Failure to manage such ignorance through probative inquiry ensures the necessity of continued control. Further, it ultimately justifies the VP or DM in blaming and replacing the store manager when store performance doesn't improve or isn't consistent, instead of requiring the executive to look in the mirror and critically examine his own sloppy approach to field leadership.

Conversely, a different set of assumptions characterizing the store manager as being uncommitted, of limited intelligence, in need of direction due to incompetence and so on, can be equally damaging and limiting if false.

In either set of assumptions the questions are disturbing. If the first set of assumptions listed above are valid, then why the need for repeated correctives? If they are invalid, then what good will more corrective direction provide? Further, if the different set of assumptions is valid, then why is this person still in position as a store manager? Why was this person hired or promoted to begin with? Why is this person still in office? What good will more corrective direction provide and at what cost to the organization if it is provided?

## COMMON MISCONCEPTIONS

Field executives are also crippled by a variety of common misconceptions that are rarely if ever challenged. Some of these misconceptions are listed below in the form of erroneous equations.

## ERRONEOUS EQUATIONS:

- *Our beliefs = The Truth*

- *Empowerment = Assigning responsibility*

- *Development = Training, telling, directing or modeling*

- *Accountability = Check-up, follow-up and feedback*

- *Assumptions = Facts*

- *Activity = Performance*

- *Confidence = Ability*

- *Compliance = Commitment*

- *Effectiveness = Getting things done*

- *Improvement = Achievement of required standards/results*

- *Potential = Performance*

- *Efforts = Results*

All these misconceptions warp the ladders of inference built upon them. They are further contaminated by our feelings that the truth is obvious, our beliefs are based on real data, and the data we select to support our beliefs are the real data.

These misconceptions and others like them, including the common and fatal misconception that our experience can be universally and uncritically applied to any problem that looks and sounds familiar, conveniently keep us trapped in old routines that don't work.

Challenging our assumptions and beliefs can be threatening, and is often resisted through defensive reasoning that too often makes our approaches to management impossible to disconfirm because of our fear of the assumed consequences of finding out we were wrong. When it is too threatening to check out our own ways of doing things, then those ways are sealed, or inaccessible, to critical, objective, public testing.

## CONSEQUENCES

The negative consequences of the DOA are extensive and significant. In addition to explaining why we persist in doing what doesn't work, they also explain why our stores and organization as a whole cannot move consistently toward greatness, and why even companies at one time touted as *excellent* or *great* have fallen from prominence.

Essentially, the defensive values, action strategies, and control-based approaches of the DOA make the organization resistant to change and make it extremely difficult for leaders to follow Jim Collins' advice (in his book *Good to Great*) to "look in the mirror" and "confront the brutal facts." Clearly, the idea that "it's all about the culture, stupid" has merit and there's no easy way around this dilemma.

Organizations infected by the DOA virus are riddled with "defensive routines." These are those "actions, policies and processes that prevent individuals or segments of the organization from experiencing embarrassment or threat" (Argyris). These defensive routines at first compromise the culture and then define it. They include how we formulate and communicate policy, how we change direction, how we structure our time and our work, how we make decisions, how we conduct our meetings, how we prepare for meetings, how we behave in meetings, how we visit stores or other operating units, how we design systems, how we structure our organization or define positions, and how we attempt to influence others to get them to change. They are characterized by action and behavior designed to save face, make a good impression, cover up bad news or hidden agendas, cover up the cover-up by making the cover-up undiscussable, and then make the fact that it is undiscussable, undiscussable.

The development we are proposing in the field and throughout all the store support functions of the organization is a work against our most basic fears and defenses. It's difficult to sustain, not because the Leadership Factor is so difficult to understand or apply, but because the alternative orientation to action it requires is unnatural to us and too threatening.

## "FANCY FOOTWORK"

Store managers and associates, as well as their VPs and DMs, are experts at a certain type of defensive maneuvering that Argyris refers to as "fancy footwork." This type of behavior, too, is designed to evade exposure and responsibility, as well as the consequences of marginal or poor performance.

Some forms of fancy footwork can be easily detected, as when someone blatantly shifts blame for their failure to perform. Other subtler forms are often missed and require a trained eye. Like all forms of control and defensive behavior, fancy footwork is undiscussable. To confront these defenses is to violate the social virtues of the DOA, something we just can't and won't do. Or maybe we can and will do it selectively, but certainly not with those in a position to harm us.

Next time you receive a non-answer to a direct question, you have witnessed fancy footwork. These non-answers come in different forms, such as *denial* ("I don't see a problem here"), *excusing* ("I don't have the resources to get it done"), *minimizing* ("It has been a lot worse"), *answers for everything* ("We tried that ...Tried that too...Tried everything"), *confusion* ("No one ever told me"), *shifting blame* ("I was told to do it differently"), and *deflection* ("I'll look into it and get back to you...We're working on it"). In one observed instance during the store visit, the store manager repeatedly changed the subject or left abruptly to attend to a customer or adjust product on a shelf that needed rearranging when the DM asked an uncomfortable accountability question. This form of fancy footwork was so natural that it was missed and therefore never confronted. The DM finally gave up and reverted back to his control-based inspection and suggestions for improvement. It was classic.

Beyond such defensiveness, the DOA has profound implications on how managers and executives approach the work of empowerment, how they respond to the idea of accountability, and how they facilitate learning in their regions, districts and stores. The defensive orientation toward empowerment involves limiting autonomy and directing instead of partnering. With accountability the emphasis is on "checking up" on people, micro-managing activity, threatening/praising, and punishing/rewarding instead of managing for results. Finally, in facilitating learning the emphasis is on reactive, experience-based learning instead of reflective, design-based learning. With such *reactive learning* there is a dependence on the thinking of, or direction from, others and an over-reliance on experience in solving complex performance problems.

## FLAWED ADVICE

Related to the DOA, flawed advice is the second explanation for why executives persist in doing what doesn't work. Flawed advice, from our perspective, includes any advice related to programs of change and development that are rooted in the DOA.

Several years ago, prior to my work in Action Science, I had extensive experience training retail executives and store managers in the habits of effective living, leadership and team building. For six consecutive years, all of the VPs, DMs, store managers and assistant store managers of a major retailer were put through three consecutive stages of rigorous, state of the art personal effectiveness training, 360 degree performance and strengths profiling, and team building courses and workshops.

Through it all we accumulated a great deal of positive evidence confirming to management and me that we were on the right track. Each year we kept building momentum.

In the seventh year, the president of the division expressed his concern that, although overall financial performance had improved consistently over the years, individual store execution was still erratic and performance was inconsistent in numerous stores, including several typically good performing stores. He noted that, based on his visits and reports, the same problems kept recurring and targeted results were not being met in every key result area of the stores in spite of ongoing store visits and the cadre of experienced RVPs, DMs and store managers in the field.

It was suggested that we stop further training and that I go out into the field and observe first-hand how the VPs and DMs were visiting stores and solving problems. This was done and to my shock, after observing numerous store visits in every region, I found no evidence that anything taught and assumedly learned by these field executives was being applied, notwithstanding all the positive feedback and assurances to the contrary received over the six years of training and teambuilding.

The most disturbing finding was that these executives really believed they had changed and were using what they had been taught. These leaders, furthermore, were passionate about their work and were considered strong leaders and a good fit according to the talents, strengths and experience they brought to their jobs. How could this be?

The training focused on the need to create trust to exercise positive influence for change. It also focused on the idea of discovering and building strengths and achieving success through the practice of allegedly well-researched habits of "highly effective people." This focus would thereby make personal weaknesses irrelevant. It turned out the advice was flawed.

Gaps between the principles of effective leadership and the practice of those principles through the recommended habits of effectiveness were not exposed or practically and realistically dealt with. These gaps included such dilemmas as how to listen to understand without listening to manipulate; how to take initiative without assuming control; how to pursue mutual benefit without manipulating the alleged benefits to the other party; how to value diversity without involving others after the fact only to get their buy-in; how to behave in "trustworthy" ways without making such behavior a means for getting what was wanted from another; or how to collaboratively empower others without abandoning them to eventually resume control.

Although some of these dilemmas were mentioned and participants were cautioned to avoid them, the cautions weren't translated to action and resulting approaches to action were never tested that dealt with these and other gaps.

The result was that action taken to create trust was inadvertently destroying trust; mixed messages were being sent between the "espoused" common language created by the advice and the actual behavior. The contradictions were covered up through defensive reasoning and fancy footwork and made undiscussable, since no one felt he could safely challenge the principles or contradictions. Finally, the undiscussability itself was made undiscussable by the collective unwillingness to expose the duplicity.

With further analysis it was also discovered that in many cases participants' strengths were also their weaknesses, and in all cases the one significant weakness they all had and couldn't manage around, because they couldn't (or wouldn't) see it, was their underlying *defensive orientation to action*. Their control-based approaches and routines were modified superficially in some cases to appear different. But in fact, they were managing the way they always had and remained victims of the fatal assumptions, self-sealing beliefs, and competing commitments that kept them stuck and unable to change.

In theory, what these executives and managers were learning about themselves and their strengths was supposed to make all their weaknesses inconsequential. It didn't. No amount of surveying, profiling or interviewing alone would have ever brought out what I saw in the field, and what we have seen since then in every other organization we have worked with.

In our experience, whether the program *du jour* is the "7 Habits of Highly Effective People," the adoption of "Principle Centered Leadership," the process of "Leading Change," the use of "Change Implementation Teams," the program of "Changing Head, Heart and Hands," the use of "Change Scorecards," or the attempt to "Discover (and capitalize on) Your Strengths," the story is always the same. Only the names of the new, latest and greatest programs have been changed. The advice, from our analysis and perspective, is still flawed and executives are seemingly buying into it uncritically because it's easy to apply, it makes sense, other companies are using it, or because they're desperate for a quick fix or an easy way out.

This experience led me to question the underlying premises of all the popular advice being advanced by authors and management experts. The question of how people learn and change has since occupied my thinking, research, and practice, and has been a motivational force for all of us in our firm. My idealistic optimism has long since given way to a more cautious realism based on an acceptance of the complexity of human nature and a natural suspicion of human motivations and of simplistic, reductive formulas for change and success.

What we have discovered is that there is no substitute for the arduous work of action learning, research, and design in facilitating sustainable change. And even in practicing this discipline of Action Science, there is the need to avoid contamination by the DOA. One of our coaches said it well as he reminded us of Freud's caution against the "rage to cure." Too often, expert advice in the pursuit of change takes on this 'rage to cure' by seeking converts to the cause, or by prescribing mind-set-changing programs that are unactionable and are, at heart, defensive and controlling in nature, in spite of what they espouse or profess.

Returning to the case above, the fact is that no one knew what was really going on until I went in the field and observed management in action. Further, the current popular programs advising executives to, for example, 'capitalize on strengths and disregard (manage around) weaknesses,' practice 'the four keys' of effective coaching, and 'engage the head, heart and hands' to cause change are, like the advice of practicing 'habits of effectiveness' above, examples of flawed advice, designed, learned, and practiced from a DOA. (For a more extensive treatment of this topic, see Argyris: *Flawed Advice and the Management Trap*, 2000, Oxford University Press.)

In addition to flawed external advice, there is flawed internal advice, which originates internally through research that is defensively structured to justify operations or preserve or extend the power base of store support functions through the advancement of a particular strategy, program or course of action. In one organization, certain stores were designated as test stores to try out new programs as potential best practices. The advocated programs were tested with favorable outcomes in top performing stores staffed with highly effective store teams.

These test stores were not representative of most of the stores in the organization, however. Consequently, the favorable results of the test were skewed in support of the programs being advocated by various store support groups, thereby furthering the agenda of the advocating support group and defensively justifying its existence or reinforcing its power within the organization. In these ways, flawed advice becomes 'best practice' that perpetuates the cycle of inconsistent performance.

Executives beware. The advice you are taking and the programs you are purchasing and implementing might be seriously flawed and defensively oriented.

## AVOIDING FLAWED ADVICE

We recommend that executives evaluate the claims and approach of any proposed development program or best practice by asking the following questions and evaluating the answers according to the guidelines suggested below:

o *How are claims tested, researched and substantiated? Valid claims are assertions supported by facts or conclusions based on action research and reason, not hearsay or testimonial evidence. While references can be informative, caution is needed to ensure that references are as specific and relevant as possible. In our experience, claims attesting to ROI or other financial improvement measures are suspect, given the extreme difficulty of isolating any one factor as the sole cause of results caused by numerous controllable and uncontrollable variables. Further, claims based on soft, anecdotal data and validated by loose, correlated connections offered as strong causal connections are not only non-evidence, they are disingenuous. This pertains to the research and evaluation of best practices as well. How, and on the basis of what assumptions, was such research structured, conducted, evaluated and interpreted?*

o *What is the underlying orientation to action implicit in the program content, or best practice, and in the nature of related profiling or evaluative instruments? Is it primarily, if not exclusively, defensive or collaborative and developmental in nature? Is there a perceived or actual gap between the espoused approach and the actual approach? If so, what mixed messages might it send and what defenses might it create or mobilize? Answering these questions requires a rigorous examination of the underlying goals, values, intentions, beliefs, and assumptions of the program content.*

o *Is the advice advocated or implied by the program actionable? Program content and best practices must be examined to ensure that the advice or practice is observable and testable, not general, vague, ambiguous or internally inconsistent. Observable actions and behavior must be clearly presented, and "gaps" in the theory must be scrupulously identified and bridged through recommended practices consistent with a truly developmental orientation.*

o *Does the learning process require "unlearning" and the application of reflective research and design-based learning interventions? Does it engage participants in real-time actual casework involving actual dilemmas encountered in the workplace? Does the structure of the learning experience allow learners to create their own content and learning experiences and to learn at their own pace? Learning structures that are rigid, formula (or habit) based, categorically simplistic, reductive (i.e. with regard to peoples personality types, strengths profiles, style categories, etc.), and presentation intensive with contrived exercises, where the primary objective is to complete the program agenda through controlled facilitation, are not conducive to action learning and sustainable change. They are not only defensively oriented, they are structurally flawed and philosophically and psychologically wrongheaded.*

## COMPETING COMMITMENTS

A third explanation for why we persist in doing what doesn't work can be found in what Kegan and Lahey refer to as the "competing commitment." (Note: See "The Real Reason People Won't Change," Robert Kegan and Lisa Lahey, Harvard Business Review, Reprint R0110E. For an extensive treatment of this topic, see Kegan and Lahey, *Seven Languages for Transformation: How the Way We Talk Can Change the Way We Work*, Jossey-Bass, 2001.)

Consider first a typical case we frequently encounter in the field. This involves a particular DM who had made the commitment to transition from the IDC approach to store visits and apply the Leadership Factor in a more developmental approach. After a while his commitment was blocked by a competing commitment to avoid a believed "worrisome outcome" of such a change. The worrisome outcome was getting fired for not doing his job. Beneath his competing commitment to not get fired were certain big assumptions that supported his conclusion that the change would be unadvisable or foolhardy. Consequently, the DM was stuck and continued to persist in doing what he knew didn't work. (More on this case later in this section.)

Here's a more wide scale example involving a dilemma experienced by one of our clients in their effort to effectuate a cultural change in their stores from a task focus to a sales and customer service focus. This company had committed to Collins' challenge of moving from "good to great." Their overall growth and performance had been consistently improving over the past two years.

About a year prior to our involvement, this company had invested considerable financial and human resources to design and roll out a comprehensive store associate selling program. This program would hopefully establish service differentiation from the competition and significantly increase sales and customer loyalty. It was to accomplish this by engaging every store manager and associate in easy, strategic interactions with the customer. These interactions were designed to serve customers and increase their purchases through up-selling. This enlarged job requirement was simple and easy to fulfill. Essentially, all the store associate needed to do was greet the customer and ask four very simple questions to determine and attend their needs. Five behaviors, that's all.

Company-wide promotions and meetings were held throughout the country and initial and periodic follow-up training programs were designed and rolled out. All associates and managers were trained, observed, "coached," encouraged and reminded. Controls were designed and put in place. Mystery shopper visits were conducted unannounced, stores were rated, and their rating affected bonuses. Additionally, VPs and DMs inspected store compliance to "get" store teams on board through recognition and reward programs, and hold them accountable for low mystery shopper and customer service scores.

By the time our firm was retained, nothing much had changed. After all that had been done and was continuing to be done to cause and reinforce compliance, execution was inconsistent at best, and no one knew why. Why was this so difficult? Why weren't associates doing these five simple things?

We were asked to work with the VPs and DMs in all four of their regions for the purpose of improving store performance. We accompanied these field executives in numerous store visits to observe them in action and work with them to design more effective approaches in developing their store managers. In the process, we encountered the dilemma of the missing five behaviors.

We discovered the existence of a common, underlying *competing commitment* that was blocking execution of this cultural change. A mixed message delivered by senior management in the context of a defensively oriented culture catalyzed strong resistance in the form of this competing commitment and mobilized in turn a variety of defensive routines and behavior.

Store associates, for the most part, saw the benefits of the change, understood its rationale and had committed to do the five behaviors. However, they also knew that they needed to maintain excellent store conditions and had experienced critical feedback from VPs, DMs, and their store managers that primarily focused on operations and store conditions. The message was mixed: "Take time to serve the customer and up-sell, keep payroll at budget, and don't let store conditions drop below standard."

In action this played out as: "The customer comes first but you better get your tasks done."

Competing with the associates' stated commitment to the cultural change and five behaviors was the competing commitment to avoid the worrisome outcome of getting in trouble for not completing the operations tasks ensuring required store conditions. Since the primary emphasis of the field executives during their control-based store visits was on inspecting and correcting store conditions (95% of time spent), and since the store managers likewise emphasized the completion of operations tasks, associates formed the big assumption that doing tasks was what was really most important.

Beneath this big assumption was the even bigger assumption that their evaluation and promote-ability or retention depended primarily on how well they did their floor tasks. And this bigger assumption led associates to the biggest assumption, that the primacy of tasks over selling was non-negotiable and undiscussable. The result: inconsistent execution and the proliferation of additional controls, defensive routines and "fancy footwork."

The common competing commitment described above was accompanied by a variety of personal competing commitments as well. The stores were swimming in them, some created as a result of a mismatch, or error of placement, or as a conflict between competing personal values or beliefs. Others, however, and far too many, resulted from the skilled sub-routine nested within every primary defensive routine we have observed.

This defensive sub-routine, which Argyris refers to as the underlying "logic" of the defensive routine itself, is skillfully constructed beneath the surface of awareness. Its exposure is often skillfully and artfully resisted through denial and defensive reasoning. The defensive "logic," according to Argyris, can be expressed in terms of four basic rules:

1. *"Craft messages that contain ambiguities or inconsistencies.*

2. *"Act as if the messages were not inconsistent.*

3. *"Make the ambiguity and inconsistency in the message undiscussable.*

4. *"Make this undiscussability undiscussable."*

When management in this case was informed of the defensive sub-routine they had built into their cultural change initiative, the initial reaction was "we'll take both, thank you very much." But the point had been missed. Management did not have to choose between customer selling and service and operational excellence. They needed to transition from a 'defensive orientation to action' to a 'collaborative orientation to action' by designing leadership approaches that employed the Leadership Factor presented in the last chapter.

They needed to see the destructive logic embedded in their defensive, control-based management approaches, especially their store visit approach, and facilitate development toward the resolution of this and other competing commitments.

How did this look? In this case, store visit routines were designed in collaboration with RVPs and select DMs to bring out the store managers' competing commitments, test the underlying assumptions, and involve the store management team in a collaborative design of those approaches that would satisfy both requirements. In those cases where this occurred, competing commitments were resolved and period results improved as predicted.

## DEEPER RESISTANCE

Often by testing and disconfirming the big assumption(s) underneath a worrisome outcome, the competing commitment is resolved. Because such disconfirmation often requires a difficult conversation, the resistance often goes deeper. The person's ability to learn and change is sometimes stopped cold by certain self-sealing beliefs that cannot be disconfirmed because the perceived level of downside risk is too high. This form of resistance is deeply rooted in the ingrained DOA and, more specifically, in the person's personality structure.

Let's return now to the earlier case involving the DM stuck in a competing commitment.

The DM continued to use the IDC approach to store visits instead of designing and adopting a more collaborative, developmental approach. He did so even though he saw the benefits of the change and sincerely wanted to make the transition.

When asked why he returned back to the IDC approach he responded by saying that his boss, the VP, really expected him to fix the stores in his district and not waste time "developing" store managers. Moreover, the DM asserted, even though the VP said he supported the developmental store visit approach, he really didn't. The VP believed the best way to develop store managers was to show them how it's done and tell them what to do and how to do it.

Enquiring deeper, it was discovered by the DM's coach that these views of the DM about the VP were assumptions inferred by the DM's interpretations of the VP's previous words and behavior. They were not currently tested or confirmed facts. When challenged to publicly test these assumptions in conversation with the VP, the DM declined. He believed it would be a waste of time and too risky to approach the VP on his behavior. To do so would expose the VP's duplicity and this would undoubtedly result in swift retaliation. Why take such a risk? The RVP would not tell the truth and would never change.

These were self-sealing beliefs. As long as they were equated with truth, the DM's assumptions about the VP would be regarded as facts and the DM's competing commitment would never be resolved. This would leave the DM stuck and persistent in using a defensive, control-based approach to store visits.

What happened here? In order to avoid the threat of loss, win and not lose, and suppress the negative emotion of frustration, the DM in this case made a defensively motivated decision to save his job and his own and the VP's face on the basis of unconfirmed beliefs and assumptions. Who lost as a result of this defensive decision and approach? Everyone, including the customer and the company.

Self-sealing beliefs are very difficult to change because: (1) they are embedded in deeply ingrained social values for winning and not losing, saving face, and avoiding the threat of losing status, esteem, security and power, and (2) they are supported by presumed knowledge, presumed because it is ultimately self-referential, e.g. "I know what I know about my boss or this situation." This is a conviction based on subjective experience of another person, not knowledge based on the actual person or situation.

This form of resistance can be confronted by labeling it for what it is and exploring the consequences of not being willing to test the underlying assumptions that support the beliefs in question. Often the outcome, however, is performance counseling, repositioning or removal. Sustained change is possible if the heat is high enough, but it is very rare in our experience, particularly in cases where the executive, manager, or associate does not have the required ego strength to risk exposure.

## SUMMARY AND CONCLUSION

In this chapter we have explored what lies at the heart of the third and final dilemma uncovered by our research: why field executives in the retail sector (or any sector!) persist in doing what doesn't work and, conversely, why they don't persist in facilitating the development of their people. At the heart of our persistence in controlling our people and our resistance to developing them through partnering and learning is a deeply embedded defensive orientation to action and leadership.

This defensive orientation is the result of extensive natural conditioning over our entire lifetime and might perhaps even be part of our very biological makeup. It is motivated primarily by the fear of failing and is continually reinforced by defensive reasoning, routines and behavior in the very organizations we work for and create through our actions and interactions. The DOA, together with its related manifestations, including the acceptance and proliferation of flawed advice and the spawning of competing commitments, can, however, be sufficiently placed in submission to a very different orientation to action. Such an alternative orientation to action allows for greater development and, as a result, for great store performance. It is, along with a very different model and approach to retail field leadership, the topic of the next chapter.

## KEY INSIGHTS FROM CHAPTER 4:

> ➤ *Underlying our persistence in doing what doesn't work is a deeply embedded defensive orientation to action which operates at the personal level, the interpersonal level, and the organizational level.*

> ➤ *The defensive orientation to action (DOA) is driven by a set of social values identified in our culture with success and happiness. These core values include setting and achieving goals, maximizing winning and minimizing losing, suppressing negative emotions, and always appearing rational by suppressing feelings.*

> ➤ *The primary action strategies related to the core values of the DOA include unilaterally designing and controlling the environment, selling and persuading others to get buy-in, owning and controlling the tasks, and unilaterally protecting self and others from exposure and embarrassment.*

> ➤ *Control-based approaches to action and leadership are motivated defensively and built on and justified by certain fatal assumptions and common misconceptions.*

> ➤ *The consequences of the DOA include the proliferation of defensive routines and fancy footwork which impede sustainable, productive change.*

> ➤ *Significant products and manifestations of the DOA include the creation and acceptance of flawed advice and the phenomenon of competing commitments.*

# CHAPTER 5

# GREAT STORE PERFORMANCE: FROM ILLUSION TO REALITY

---

*In this Chapter:*

➤ *What's the alternative to the DOA and the inspect/direct/correct approach to store visits?*

➤ *How can we consistently employ the Leadership Factor in our store visits to make them truly developmental and thereby "solve the right problems in the right way"?*

➤ *What's wrong with our 'good' performing stores?*

➤ *Why is centralized Store Support more hindrance than support and how can that change?*

---

Inconsistent and mediocre-to-good store performance will continue to be the lot of even the biggest and best retail organizations as long as their field executives continue to employ defensively oriented, control-based approaches to leadership, and also as long as store support functions within the organization, along with the VPs and DMs, continue to run the stores behind the scenes and reduce store managers to the role of mindless, underpowered operators.

For many retailers, 'good' store performance on average would be perfectly acceptable. We won't argue with that. However, for those few retailers who aspire to great store performance as a means to market advantage and who agreed with Collins that "the good is the enemy of the great," good is simply not good enough.

So perhaps we have yet one more dilemma to consider in this final chapter. If our leaders and associates are trapped inside a box and the instructions for getting out of the box are written on the outside of the box, how do we get out?

We propose that there is a way out because there is an alternative mental model, a different orientation to action than the DOA. Before we present this alternative, however, we need to administer another dose of reality in hope of disabusing you of yet one more fatal illusion.

Seeing the truth of our condition is not enough to ensure change. In addition to our own research and experience over a period of nearly thirty years, there is the research of our various colleagues working in other sectors and organizations that confirm what we've known since 1975. Specifically, in regard to making sustainable change, we know:

> *Learning about our errors or deficiencies by listening to lectures, reading books, or doing exercises or constructed case work is not enough.*

> *Learning about these problems through personalized research, actual results and diagnostic findings is not enough.*

> *Participating in periodic training courses, teambuilding sessions, and executive retreats are likewise not enough.*

> *Attending motivational rallies, 'successful living' retreats and unilaterally practicing new habits of effectiveness are not enough.*

> *Receiving corrective feedback and 360 degree profiling are not enough.*

> *Operant conditioning through performance reviews and structured recognition and reward are not enough.*

> *Doing any combination of the above, either in sequence or concurrently, is not enough.*

The above approaches, though helpful to some degree if not inherently flawed, will not produce anything other than temporary improvement in behavior and an attitude of compliance. The question is why not? And the answer is we don't know completely.

It seems that at some level there is strategic value in believing, acting and reacting defensively as we do. What would such strategic value consist of? At least three things: (1) survival and success through our avoidance of exposure and the anxiety of failure; (2) evidence to justify our defensive patterns and routines and the perceptions and beliefs that produced them; and (3) personal satisfaction in being "right" about others when they respond reactively to our provocations. These and other valued benefits tend to keep us in the DOA in spite of our best efforts and intentions.

To result in sustainable change, our action research shows that behavior and approaches to action used by executives and managers must first be observed and recorded by qualified coaches. They must then be openly exposed to those observed. Next, leaders must be engaged in a reflective form of learning. Such learning would proceed at their own pace and will enable them to deepen their self-awareness and collaboratively design, test, and apply new approaches and solutions under a different set of governing values and assumptions.

There must be, additionally, real-time feedback from coaches supported by valid information. And there must be effective *horizontal inquiry* (what? when? who?) and deeper *vertical inquiry* (what? why? how?) to explore and understand relevant contexts, meanings, intentions, motives, and assumptions to promote self-reflection. Last, but not least, there must be sufficient self-imposed pressure to learn and change. No pain, no change.

These arduous requirements go far beyond traditional forms of classroom training and education. And they also go far beyond control-based feedback provided defensively to get others to change.

The type of partnering and reflective, design-based learning presented and advocated in Chapter 3 is the only way we are aware of (barring psychotherapy) that will enable us to successfully transition from the DOA master program to its alternative. This means, at the store level, field executives must consistently apply the Leadership Factor in every developmental conversation they have with store managers. Further, they must decisively upgrade their district store manager teams when development is being frustrated through prolonged and immovable resistance to change.

In this final chapter we will first propose an alternative mental model to the DOA and then present in some detail a radically different approach to field leadership. We will suggest, in keeping with the counsel in Chapter 2 to "solve the right problem in the right way," that DMs facilitate the development of store mangers through the conversational application of the Leadership Factor presented in Chapter 3. This would be done through what we term a developmental store visit that focuses on the store manager as the root problem of all controllable store problems.

Consistent with the idea that "the good is the enemy of the great" (Collins), we will also address the problem of the "good" performing store by probing deeply into hidden vulnerabilities masked by surface performance indicators.

Finally, we will suggest the idea of "Store Support" embraced by numerous retailers has become an oxymoron. We will assert that store support functions are defensive and intrusive, inadvertently undermining store performance. We will explore the built-in tensions between the stores and the store support functions and call for meaningful dialogue to resolve these tensions in order to foster performance accountability and "great" performance.

But first, let's go back to the first requirement to transition from the DOA. What do we transition to?

## THE ALTERNATIVE

The alternative to the Defensive Orientation to Action (DOA) is what Argyris refers to as "Model II" and which we refer to as the Collaborative Orientation to Action (COA). This alternative mental model and theory of action focuses on development and engagement. Whereas the DOA exists in each of us instinctually and through deep social conditioning, the COA must be learned. And not just learned, but consciously factored into our approaches and practiced continuously.

While we would argue that the COA produces better decisions and better serves the organization and our higher needs for social contribution and self-actualization, it is not primary. To take root in any organization, an interdependent level of maturity by a sufficient number of people is required. Further, and perhaps most importantly, such an orientation must be embraced and supported by senior management. Such maturity and support enables people to serve their own self-interests through mutual collaboration and creative negotiation.

For many, the COA does not come quickly and can easily be counterfeited, and often is. This orientation for action is driven by the needs for contribution and actualization and the corresponding values for: (1) valid information; (2) informed and voluntary decisions; (3) internalized commitment; (4) risk, learning and accomplishment; (5) diversity of thought and perspective; and (6) adult interactions that include the authentic expression of views and feelings. These values, as you recall, are vastly different from the core values inherent in the DOA, which operate primarily out of a dependent level of maturity and which strive for unilateral control of the environment and others to avoid the threat of exposure, embarrassment and loss.

The schematic below shows the relationships among the governing values of the COA and the corresponding action strategies and consequences to performance and learning.

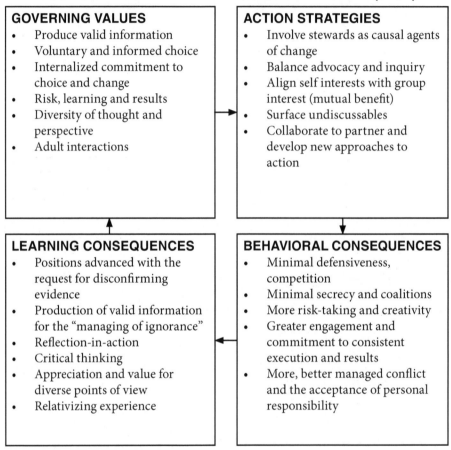

## COLLABORATIVE ORIENTATION TO ACTION (COA)

**GOVERNING VALUES**
- Produce valid information
- Voluntary and informed choice
- Internalized commitment to choice and change
- Risk, learning and results
- Diversity of thought and perspective
- Adult interactions

**ACTION STRATEGIES**
- Involve stewards as causal agents of change
- Balance advocacy and inquiry
- Align self interests with group interest (mutual benefit)
- Surface undiscussables
- Collaborate to partner and develop new approaches to action

**LEARNING CONSEQUENCES**
- Positions advanced with the request for disconfirming evidence
- Production of valid information for the "managing of ignorance"
- Reflection-in-action
- Critical thinking
- Appreciation and value for diverse points of view
- Relativizing experience

**BEHAVIORAL CONSEQUENCES**
- Minimal defensiveness, competition
- Minimal secrecy and coalitions
- More risk-taking and creativity
- Greater engagement and commitment to consistent execution and results
- More, better managed conflict and the acceptance of personal responsibility

Notice the differences between the contents of each box of the above COA schematic and the DOA schematic below.

# DEFENSIVE ORIENTATION TO ACTION (DOA)

| GOVERNING VALUES | ACTION STRATEGIES |
|---|---|
| • Set goals and achieve them<br>• Maximize winning, minimize losing<br>• Suppress negative thoughts/ emotions<br>• Always appear rational<br>• Uphold the hierarchy<br>• Suppress feelings, save face, keep everyone happy | • Unilaterally design and control the environment<br>• Sell, persuade, manipulate outcomes<br>• Own and control the task<br>• Protect one's self (cover up) and others<br>• Bypass undiscussables |
| **LEARNING CONSEQUENCES**<br>• Self-reinforcing arguments<br>• Self-referential reasoning<br>• Self-sealing approaches<br>• Private validation of inferences<br>• Increased frustration and dilemma<br>• Dependence on the thinking of, or direction from, others<br>• Over-reliance on experience | **BEHAVIORAL CONSEQUENCES**<br>• Defensiveness, CYA, cover-up, competitiveness, blaming others<br>• Political gamesmanship<br>• Conformity, groupthink, distancing, minimal risk-taking<br>• Inconsistent performance<br>• Compliance at the expense of commitment<br>• Distortion of key information<br>• Create defensive routines |

These two orientations to action can be further contrasted as we compare the actions and behavior of the COA below with those presented in the previous chapter.

Some examples of COA actions or behavior:

- *Focus on "team" and "management"-level performance problems that impede effective execution and results.*

- *Confront the brutal facts, including personal attitudes and behaviors, to face subsurface assumptions and beliefs.*

- *Advocate a position and balance it with inquiry and self-reflection.*

- *Speak or inquire in directly observable ways, using valid information, to enable individuals to confront inconsistencies in their reasoning and behavior and incongruities between their intended and actual actions.*

- *Advocate principles, values, and beliefs in a way that invites inquiry and encourages other people to do the same.*

Looking deeper at a more personal level, consider the following descriptive sentence completions, which further illustrate the COA mindset and related actions and behavior:

"You know you are operating out of the Collaborative Orientation to Action (COA) when, generally speaking...

- *your intention in engaging others to resolve performance problems is to discover and explore collaboratively, in a spirit of curiosity and concern, the status of and needs for empowerment and learning*

- *you seek to produce valid information, through observation and probative inquiry, to make informed business decisions and developmental decisions regarding building and upgrading the team*

- *you create the conditions for internal commitment by working with your reporting partners to enable them to critically explore and analyze existing actions and create and test new approaches through reflective learning*

- *you realize that your reporting partners' motivation and commitment are not caused by you directly; rather, they come from within them as a derivative of their personal choices and success in learning and creating something of value to them and the organization*

- *you balance advocacy and inquiry to produce valid information and ensure the best thinking for decisions*

- *you respectfully check out with others your concerns in different performance and accountability conversations and discuss the undiscussables*

- *you engage others on an "adult-to-adult" level, not on a "parent-to-child" basis, and thereby annul the requirements of the implicit "parental contract" to protect, coddle, secure, and provide for their emotional needs for acceptance and approval."*

This alternative orientation to action, again, does not come naturally to people, which explains the prevalence of counterfeit collaborative and developmental approaches to action.

## COUNTERFEIT APPROACHES TO COLLABORATIVE ACTION AND DEVELOPMENT

Counterfeit approaches to collaborative, developmental leadership are simply DOA approaches disguised as COA approaches. Their intention and action must first be distinguished from what we have earlier referred to as the "gap" between intended and actual approaches to action. My actual approach to action might be incongruent with my intended, or planned, approach without the approach itself being counterfeit. The counterfeit approach is much more than a performance error.

Rather, a counterfeit approach is presented as being one thing while in reality being something else. While it appears to be collaborative in nature, it is actually defensive and driven by an underlying intent to control.

There are many examples of counterfeit developmental store visits in the field where VPs and DMs, like our DM in Chapter 1, use certain recommended "coaching" techniques and motivational leadership tactics to control their store managers' performance. For example, numerous field executives have admitted to using positive encouragement, praise and supportive behavior to engage their store manager. They see this as empowering change. It is really parental control and manipulation disguised as empowerment.

We also see counterfeit approaches at the highest levels of management. One example involves a new CEO of a large retailer who, out of concern for heavy cost structure, the defeated culture, and the corresponding lack of employee engagement, took action that appeared to be very developmental. He first de-layered the store's organization to cut costs. He then set up multi-disciplinary "change teams" charged with the task of aligning company-wide performance management systems with the "shared values" he had established.

These change teams were also charged to meet with different departments throughout the company to lay out the "shared vision and values" and inform employees of the behaviors expected. Concurrently, Human Resources was instructed to cut benefits costs, modify the compensation system to lower payroll costs, and initiate a mandatory company-wide training program to improve employee engagement and morale.

On the surface, the strategic initiatives were intended to be developmental, with the CEO getting management and employees involved in the changes he thought needed to be made. The CEO's stated goal was to improve profitability and performance, and he set out to achieve that goal by: (1) de-layering and reducing benefits and payroll costs; (2) increasing responsibility through enlarged spans of management; (3) changing behaviors by informing and selling benefits of the required changes to employees to get buy-in; (4) aligning the performance system with core values; and (5) increasing employee engagement and morale through mandatory training. All of this he was doing for the good of the company and its people.

But a closer look at the CEO's actual approaches to moving his agenda forward were anything but collaborative. He had taken control of the environment and of the decision process. He had sold his program through strong advocacy without challenge and had mandated behavioral compliance and program attendance. He did so by assuming that he knew what was best for "his" people. While appearing to be sensitive to other views by soliciting their participation and involvement, he simultaneously sent the message that he had already made up his mind, and the only choice was to get on board or leave.

Nor was the CEO's program "developmental." There was no empowerment or design-based learning going on. In the stores' organization, enlarged spans of management led to increased control as leaders continued to use the IDC approach to survive. The name of the game was survival in certain regions of the business as field executives continued to take control of the stores. Further, the mandatory training did not engage participants in the kind of learning that would result in internal commitment. There was no action research and design built into the program. The training was designed to inspire participants by teaching them how to be more effective in their personal lives and interactions in the workplace. It was intended to create an attitude adjustment.

The CEO's entire approach was control-based and driven by the DOA. Needless to say, the CEO's counterfeit approach dug a deeper hole, creating counterfeit engagement and unsustainable performance improvement.

In another example with a different retailer, the president, the victim of flawed advice, mandated that every store executive team participate in an intensive one week developmental team-building program. This program was designed to build trust and improve teamwork and store performance throughout the entire company. It required members of each team to assess and reveal their own personal leadership style, teaching them how to flex their personal style in working with others to get their cooperation. It also required them to solicit and share "stop/start/continue" suggestions with members of their team to build understanding and trust. It instructed participants on techniques for communicating with each other to get buy-in. And it required team members to share and own the results of their personal 360 degree profile publicly and commit to change. Through this program, management would supposedly be able to get team members to better cooperate and work together as a team.

On the surface, this approach, like the one in the previous case, was developmental. But again, the fact that it was mandated, that everyone had to participate and that the underlying intention was to make people more cooperative, self-aware, and flexible to improve teamwork and store performance by getting them to share to build trust made it a counterfeit developmental initiative.

In both of the above cases, the executive presumed to know best what his people needed. And in both cases the strategies and programs were control-based. Consequently, the outcomes in both organizations were sadly ironic.

In the first case, the very attitudes of engagement the CEO hoped to ignite in the employee base were used to cover up non-performance and the expected values-based behaviors were never realized. In the face of the CEO's and management's defensive routines, employee behavior became highly politicized fancy footwork to avoid confrontation and accountability. This effectively shut down strong collaboration, making necessary dissent, disagreement, and challenge increasingly synonymous with negativity. Undercover cynicism became malignant as positive attitudes gave way to reality. Initial optimism dissipated under the relentless pressures of a culture of fear, driven by the DOA.

In the second case, the enthusiastic pursuit of high-performance teams turned to counterfeit optimism. Short-term gains weren't sustained to match longer-term run rates and, when increased trust, cooperation, and team synergy did not translate into high-performance, the hammer fell. People got fired, and the illusion of trust evaporated.

Some might interject at this point that, since performance can always improve, everything we do in managing others involves trying to get people to improve.

The point is that from the COA we value the "voluntary, informed choice" of each person: *their* informed choice to partner, *their* informed choice to own the offered and negotiated stewardship, *their* informed choice to be accountable according to the terms and conditions of the PPA or company requirements, *their* informed choice to learn, change and improve their performance, *their* informed choice to develop and function as responsible adults, *their* informed choice to work with others. These realities, imposed by the core values of the COA, redefine your choices as a leader and the managing partner of the various partnerships in the organization that comprise your stewardship.

Your choices and actions as a leader are all circumscribed, we would suggest, by one overarching mandate. This mandate has two parts: (1) *to collaboratively produce valid information to make the best informed business decisions possible regarding the requirements of your stewardship, and (2) to manage execution for results by appropriately applying the Leadership Factor to the right performance problems at the right level in the problem pyramid. This requires collaboratively developing and upgrading your team for optimal performance through ongoing partnering and reflective, design-based learning and problem solving.*

In other words, your most effective choices and actions are governed and driven by the goals, core values, and corresponding intentions of the COA. They are arrived at through the collaborative action strategies and approaches of the COA, not the goals, core values, and corresponding intentions, action strategies and control-based approaches of the DOA.

How to design such collaborative and developmentally-based approaches is the domain of Action Science and one primary objective of Action Science-based field coaching and action learning.

What's common with all of the counterfeit approaches and "leadership development" programs listed above, as well as any change or development effort engaged in defensively, is the *underlying intent*. The intent of 'getting others' to do what "you" want them to do, think what "you" want them to think, or buy-in to "your" agenda or point of view is the problem. A person might not be aware of such an underlying intention, but it will certainly influence, if not determine, the actions they take nonetheless. And it will do so even if they genuinely embrace and profess allegiance to collaboration and development.

What we are suggesting is that to ensure the best decisions for the company, passionate advocacy must be balanced with an equally passionate commitment to inquiry and dissent. This requires dialogue, discussion, and debate to ensure the validity and soundness of the decision process and content through strong, high-level collaboration and commitment to action.

Because of the primacy of the DOA, it is easy for executives, prone to taking control, to deceive themselves into believing that they are operating out of a COA when they are not. This reality presents another compelling reason why we think executive and field coaching, as well as the critical evaluation of advice and change initiatives, are so crucial to the transition process. The executive coach, certified in the discipline of applied Action Science, knows what to look for and how to act as a mirror to the client and to their advisors. This enables them to see what they otherwise cannot or will not see and to unlearn DOA approaches and design COA approaches.

## THE WAY OUT: BREAKING THE CONTROL CYCLE AND ACHIEVING GREAT STORE PERFORMANCE THROUGH APPLIED ACTION SCIENCE

The transition process from the DOA to the COA will, in fact, occur through *the consistent application of the Leadership Factor*. This will entail, as we shall shortly see, one developmental conversation at a time - one partnering conversation, one accountability conversation and one learning, problem-solving and decision-making conversation at a time. These developmental conversations, we suggest, will occur between the store manager and his or her managing partner, primarily within the framework of periodic store visits. Such store visits, from the COA, will no longer be control-based, defensive routines. Instead they will be collaborative, developmental problem-solving interventions. They are conducted by the DM with the store manager and designed to resolve high-leverage *team* and *management problems* related to store performance.

In Chapter 1 we learned that the prevailing theory of retail field leadership translated to what we termed the 'inspect/direct/correct' (IDC) approach to store visits. As you recall, this control-based approach is a supervisor-driven, defensive routine, a by-product of the governing DOA we learned about in Chapter 4. Through its continued use, retail organizations have continued to experience a variety of undesirable and unwanted results. We also learned in Chapter 2 that this IDC approach focuses the efforts of the store team on presenting and process level problems, neglecting the root problem and highest level opportunity. It neglects the store manager's inability to apply the Leadership Factor to build and upgrade a high-performance store team from the COA.

## A NEW APPROACH TO RETAIL FIELD LEADERSHIP

In contrast, a collaborative, developmental approach to retail field leadership focuses the VP on the DM's development and the DM on the store manager's development. We have labeled this the *Observe/Inquire/ Develop* (OID) approach to field leadership. It has been designed and tested in alternative store visits with numerous VPs and DMs over the years and with positive results.

Below is a schematic of the OID approach, which we invite you to compare at this time with the schematic of the IDC approach found in Chapter 1, page 25.

## OBSERVE/INQUIRE/DEVELOP APPROACH TO STORE IMPROVEMENT

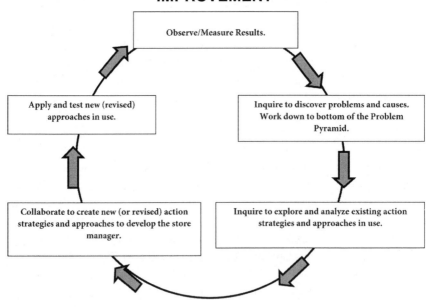

Observe/Measure Results.

Apply and test new (revised) approaches in use.

Inquire to discover problems and causes. Work down to bottom of the Problem Pyramid.

Collaborate to create new (or revised) action strategies and approaches to develop the store manager.

Inquire to explore and analyze existing action strategies and approaches in use.

This approach has its own rationale, which corresponds with the core values of the COA presented earlier. They are as follows:

## RATIONALE FOR CHANGE

The "observe, inquire, and develop" approach to retail field leadership:

- *Facilitates the acquisition of valid information and strategic perspective in relation to problems and opportunities for improvement.*

- *Enables leaders to manage their ignorance and make free, informed choices. Through this approach, field executives are able to see what store managers see and don't see and help them reflect on what they are doing and not doing and why.*

- *Tests others' understanding and degree of internal commitment regarding expectations, delegated stewardships, and accountabilities.*

- *Confronts and overcomes resistance, organizational defenses, and competing commitments that might undermine change and performance.*

- *Ensures thinking and development for improved and sustained performance/execution.*

To make this approach actionable we have designed and tested different store visit protocols or processes. One such process is presented below for your consideration and use.

Our intent in offering this approach and its corresponding store visit process is to provide a new vision of retail field management that we think will facilitate great store performance. Our purpose is not to circumvent the learning process, but to stimulate it. This isn't the only way to visit stores. It is *a* way. It is reasonable to assert that there are many effective ways for field executives to visit stores developmentally within the strategic constructs of the COA. As a field executive, you are limited only by your own curiosity, imagination and personal insecurities.

The developmental store visit approach presented below is based on the action research we have performed to date and seems consistent with the COA as a more developmental, collaborative approach to action. Further, and crucially, it applies all three fundamentals of the Leadership Factor at the right level of the Problem Pyramid.

Before attempting to use the following store visit process, it will be very important to heed the special caution included at the conclusion of its presentation. It will also be important to keep in mind the previous discussion regarding counterfeit COA approaches to action. With all this in mind, let's proceed.

## NEW DEVELOPMENTAL STORE VISIT PROCESS: INTRODUCTION

The focus of this developmental store visit process is, again, on the store manager, not the store. We recommend that the field executive adopt an attitude of productive indifference toward the store itself and instead focus with laser precision on the performance and development of the store manager. This concentrates the field executive on the highest-leverage problem or opportunity for improvement and the two overarching objectives presented in Chapter 2. For convenience, these two objectives are repeated below for your review:

> **OBJECTIVE #1:** *Develop the store manager's ability to consistently and effectively address team performance problems by building and upgrading the store team in a way that will foster more consistently effective execution.*

> **OBJECTIVE #2:** *Produce valid information regarding the store manager's ability and desire in building and upgrading the store team for the purpose of determining what changes, if any, need to be made to build and upgrade the district store management team.*

Such a focus on the store manager, and on store management performance problems in particular, is rooted in the COA presented earlier. Specifically, the store visit process that follows engages the DM and store manager initially in problem discovery and exploration down the "problem pyramid." Additionally, as mentioned earlier, it incorporates three types of developmental conversations that correspond to the three fundamentals of the Leadership Factor presented in Chapter 3. As suggested in Chapter 2, such an approach is, in our view, the 'right (or best) way to address the right (or root) problem' related to erratic execution and inconsistent store performance.

The three types of developmental conversations referenced above are as follows:

## PARTNERING CONVERSATIONS

*These conversations establish and maintain baseline empowerment as the basis of accountability and the context for the store manager's development.*

## ACCOUNTABILITY CONVERSATIONS

*These conversations focus on the reporting and fulfillment of the store manager's stewardship, as well as his capability and attitude.*

## LEARNING CONVERSATIONS

*These conversations facilitate the development of the store manager and his ability to effectively lead and upgrade his team.*

# SCHEMATIC:
## THREE DEVELOPMENTAL CONVERSATIONS

**Partnering/Empowering**
**Conversations**

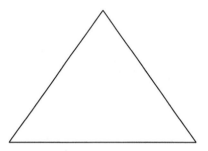

**Accountability**          **Learning**
**Conversations**          **Conversations**

Let's explore each conversation type in more depth.

## PARTNERING CONVERSATIONS

These are used to establish, revise, or revisit the baseline partnership understanding, or PPA, as the basis for accountability and development in the relationship.

In partnering conversations, a DM and a store manager might also address issues such as:

> ➤ *The basis the partners will be using in evaluating the store manager's performance.*

> ➤ *How and when the store manager will update the DM on store performance or specific results.*

> ➤ *How often the DM will visit the store and what those visits will consist of.*

## ACCOUNTABILITY CONVERSATIONS

Accountability conversations provide a joint assessment of performance and a forum for both partners to account for their performance as agreed in the PPA. This could include:

> *Exploration of causes and possible changes associated with performance or non-performance issues and concerns.*

> *Exploration of limiting factors and vulnerability associated with each partner's performance or non-performance.*

> *Exploration and determination of consequences associated with each partner's performance or non-performance.*

These conversations occur periodically with each period's results as well as annually in formal performance appraisals, or as otherwise planned and needed. They are absolutely essential to ensuring great store performance.

## LEARNING CONVERSATIONS

Learning conversations ultimately result not only in improved store and district performance and results, but also in greater engagement and internal commitment on the part of both parties. For these reasons these conversations need to occur in *every* store visit. As learning conversations are designed to facilitate a change in the store manager's orientation and action, they are developmental in a unique way.

In learning conversations, the DM works with the store manager through a process we referred to in Chapter 3 as *reflective learning and problem solving.* The objective of these conversations is to engage the store manager in effectively identifying and resolving process and execution problems within his or her team. This is accomplished through the research and design of his own approaches to empowerment, accountability, decision-making and team learning.

There are different ways of doing this. One way, which is presented below, involves the DM observing the store manager in action with his managers in the first two of a three stage learning intervention. These first two stages provide the developmental context for the third stage of this particular intervention, which involves both the DM and the store manager in a learning conversation aimed at store manager development and the resolution of team performance problems. Each stage of this prescribed learning intervention is a separate learning conversation. Let's take a look at this particular learning intervention, recognizing again that it is merely one way of many.

## THE THREE STAGE LEARNING INTERVENTION

The DM first instructs the store manager on the process and rationale for the first two stages of this learning intervention. Then the two partners work collaboratively to design a facilitation approach for use by the store manager. To do so the DM can use the coaching process presented on pages 94-98. The intent here is for the store manager to facilitate stages one and two with the DM observing the store manager and team in action.

> **STAGE ONE:** *This conversation usually involves the store manager and the store manager's management team in the exploration of one or two of the most pressing presenting problems facing the store. Together the store manager explores with his team what the problem is, if it is recurring in nature, what has been done to deal with the presenting problem and why, and what results have occurred or are anticipated given the action planned or taken.*

> **STAGE TWO:** *In this conversation the store manager explores with his team which core processes are relevant to the presenting problem, who owns those processes, and whether or not they are in place and being effectively utilized. Finally, any errors or deficiencies in examined processes need to be resolved by the store manager and team working together, with collaborative input from the field executive(s) present as needed. This level of problem solving, if collaborative and developmental, will exhibit the effective balancing of advocacy and inquiry in presenting, exploring, and evaluating options.*

> *In Chapter 2, we listed some questions that would help the DM better assess the extent to which there is a process-related breakdown in the store. Some of these questions include:*

> ➢ *What processes are relevant to this presenting problem?*

➤ *Are the processes actually in place in the store?*

➤ *Are the people trained in the processes?*

➤ *Are the processes themselves effective or do they need to be modified to be effective?*

➤ *Do the processes provide valid information that enable people to make effective decisions?*

➤ *Are they supportive of the company's strategies and programs?*

➤ *Are they aligned with the realities of the business?*

*Remember, this is a process of collaborative discovery and exploration. It is designed to produce valid information as a basis for enabling the store manager and his management team to take appropriate corrective action aimed at the root of a potential problem.*

*The approach the store manager uses in this inquiry is critical to its success. He should first be instructed by the DM, as directed above, in the guidelines for effective inquiry (Appendix A) and the coaching process of problem solving and collaboration presented in Chapter 3. He then needs to carefully position, beforehand, the learning conversation with his managers as an opportunity to explore possibilities and to uncover potential root-level problems.*

*As the problem-solving process proceeds and answers to the questions come forward, those answers are explored in more depth and validated. Underlying assumptions need to be brought to the surface and explored for their soundness through more targeted inquiry, exploring the "hows" and "whys" of answers given. This dialogue is, yet again, intended to be collaborative and developmental in nature. It is not about the store manager (or DM) coming up with the right answers. It is about joint exploration and resolution of the problem.*

*Too often, when a store manager is unskilled at this approach, the store management team sees the questions as being accusatory or threatening. This should not be an interrogation, or even an interview. It is critical for the store manager to position this conversation properly, focus on its developmental purpose and approach it collaboratively from a genuine attitude of curiosity. In this conversation, the store manager is attempting to facilitate learning and problem solving and minimize defensiveness. He needs to be on the lookout for scripted or superficial answers to the questions, which are simply being thrown out in order to get through the meeting.*

*Additionally, as part of this second stage of this learning intervention, the DM carefully observes the store manager and his management team in action as they walk the sales floor and back rooms, noting the nature of the interactions and the effectiveness of the process. Specifically, the DM needs to discover which problems are being identified or missed, how they are being addressed, and whether or not the store team is being effectively developed and empowered.*

**STAGE THREE:** *The DM works with the store manager privately on the process and execution problems that emerged in the first two stages. The two partners collaborate to uncover and address the design opportunities that surfaced during the learning and problem-solving conversation, including the walkthrough with the store team. Then together they identify and formulate potential partnering, learning, and accountability conversations that the store manager needs to have with his own team members.*

*In this third stage, most DMs have an almost inherent predisposition to shift into the "direct" and "correct" modes of the IDC approach. It is so easy for them to list the five or six biggest problems they saw during the walkthrough, for example, and to prescribe the corrective action that needs to occur. Obviously, this temptation must be avoided.*

*This stage is where development of the highest and most significant level occurs in the DM/store manager relationship. It is where the DM and the store manager work together, as partners, to address the store manager's and his team's developmental opportunities. Further, it is where the DM can work with the store manager to design improved ways for the store manager to regularly and systematically observe store conditions and team performance and engage in developmental problem solving.*

Such learning conversations also produce the information necessary for the other two developmental conversations concerning partnering and accountability. This is the critical information that can be used to upgrade the district's store management team.

These learning conversations are integral to furthering the level of internal commitment the store manager feels toward his role and the success of his team and the organization. Leaders need to realize that they can't get people committed. Such a defensive goal is an illusion, and anyone who seriously believes it is deluded.

Commitment is an internal attitude that evolves through the experience of personal success through applied learning. Direct reports can cultivate internalized commitment through their own personal learning and the success they experience through that learning.

There are times, of course, when the DM encounters resistance to learning or to change or when, as presented in the last chapter, the store manager's stated commitment to change does not materialize due to some competing commitment.

## CONVERSATIONAL DESIGN

Before the DM engages the store manager in any of the three developmental conversations, we suggest meeting with either a qualified peer or certified coach, or the coached and educated VP, to collaborate on the design of the conversations. The following conversational design process is very similar in logic and structure to the coaching methodology we've been advocating and referring to above.

## CONVERSATIONAL DESIGN PROCESS:

1. *Determine the purpose of the conversation, as well as possible biases related to existing beliefs and assumptions about the store manager. Be very clear and honest here. If you are coming from the DOA, revise the purpose, objective and intent to the COA, making them developmental rather than defensive. If such a transition is resisted, you might be dealing with a competing commitment or a crisis in confidence in the store manager or in yourself that needs to be addressed first.*

2. *From the developmental purpose develop the steps in the progression of the conversation. Given what you want to accomplish, how might you approach the conversation? How do you envision the conversation unfolding? What's the agenda you need to pursue in this particular intervention? Test your agenda against the COA.*

3. *Map out the conversation using a two-column format. In the right-hand column (RHC) build the anticipated conversation as you imagine it unfolding between you and the store manager. Write how you might start the conversation, followed by how the store manager might respond, followed by what you could say, followed by the other's response and so on. Let your agenda guide your conversation and your knowledge of the store manager determine his or her likely response. As you imagine and write down a likely response to your question or comment, note your reactions to the store manager's responses in the left-hand column (LHC). As you continue to map out the conversation, bring the LHC thoughts and concerns to the RHC through restatement and appropriate questions to test and confirm your understanding. Let the conversation proceed naturally while remaining mindful of its intended purpose. If digressions are necessary, take them or note them to be addressed later or in a different conversation. Stay on course.*

4. *After mapping out the conversation on paper, walk through the design with your coach or partner. Test for mixed messages, defensiveness, control, and collaboration. Also test for appropriate LHC work during the conversation. Finally, test for the accomplishment of the developmental objective.*

5. *Modify the design as needed to better reflect the COA, accomplish the developmental objective, and adjust for LHC influences. Test the revised design against the objective and related criteria for success.*

6. *Role-play to further test the design in action. Make final adjustments to the design. This finalized design is your intended approach and it should be collaborative and developmental in nature and in intent. After the conversation takes place, return to step #3 above and map out the "actual" conversation with both columns completed for further analysis and redesign in the context of steps 1 and 2.*

The above process is called for in those cases where the DM is engaging the store manager in a high-leverage, crucial conversation. Initially, the design process is time consuming and cumbersome and requires expert coaching. Over time, the process becomes internalized and the leader will be able to leverage his experience and increased awareness to design the conversations in less time, without a coach and with greater effectiveness. In the beginning, however, we again recommend the use of a coach and a rigorous application of the process as prescribed. (Note: There are various resources available to the executive on the subject of conversational design. Two that we recommend are *Difficult Conversations* by Stone, Patton and Heen (2000), published by Penguin Books, and *Crucial Conversations* by Patterson, Grenny, McMillan and Switzler (2002), published by McGraw Hill.)

We are now ready to incorporate all three developmental conversations into the developmental store visit process referred to earlier. This seven-step process essentially involves only the DM and the store manager. Beyond observing the store manager walking the sales floor with his team, this process need not always involve observation of the store manager engaged in developmental conversations with his managers, although it can and, at times, should.

We suggest that field executives observe their reporting partners in action as frequently as possible. Hearsay accounts by store managers regarding how their partnering, accountability, and learning conversations went with their managers are a poor substitute for direct observation.

## THE SEVEN-STEP DEVELOPMENTAL STORE VISIT PROCESS

The first four steps of this process involve an interactive exchange between the DM and the store manager as they both move down the problem pyramid. The last three steps of the process involve both the DM and the store manager in reflective learning, accountability, and partnering conversations, as presented and illustrated in Chapter 3. (Note: For an expanded treatment of the *reflective learning* intervention process, see Appendix B to this chapter.)

An alternative process to the one suggested below is presented in Appendix C to this chapter. This alternative "three stage visit" process was initially designed in 2001 and tested in different organizations. It was supplanted by the less structured "seven step process" in 2006.

The intended structure of the conversations corresponding to each step of the seven-step process is intentionally not provided. Utilizing the conversation design process presented earlier, along with the content presented above and in Chapter 3 regarding the nature of the three types of developmental conversations, the field executive and coach (or partner) can work together to co-create the action strategies and conversations that become the "actionable" content of the store visit process. This will be an invaluable developmental exercise for the field executives involved.

# DEVELOPMENTAL STORE VISIT PROCESS

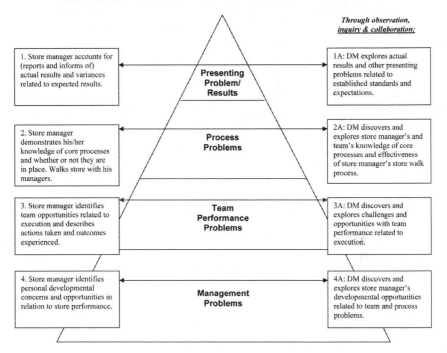

5. DM and store manager jointly determine which team performance problem(s) need to be addressed.

6. DM coaches and collaborates with the store manager using the reflective learning process to design and test solutions to selected team performance problem(s).

7. DM and store manager address store manager's performance and development needs in relation to their PPA and modify the PPA as needed.

## THE RECAP

At the end of the developmental store visit, which includes all three crucial conversations in the seven-step process above, we suggest a reflective recap. The purpose of the recap is for both partners to discuss the developmental experience, reflect on learnings, and explore together further developmental needs and next steps moving forward.

The recap is not intended to be a parental exercise in making sure the store manager follows through and does something with the designed solutions. The choice to apply learnings is the store manager's, not the DM's or VP's. This developmental recap is not defensive or control-based. The field executive would not, for example, require the store manager to make any time or process commitments or prepare any action plans. Neither the store visit nor the recap is designed to make the field executive feel better or more secure. Certainly, the managing partner will manage his stewardship for results. Also, the PPA can be reviewed as part of the visit, and separate partnering and accountability conversations might be required as specified in the seven-step process. *But not in the recap.* The focus of the recap is on mutual learnings.

Given the above, some appropriate recap questions might include:

> ➤ *What did we learn from our conversations today about . . .*

>> o *The store?*

>> o *The store team?*

>> o *Ourselves, individually and as partners?*

> ➤ *What vulnerabilities, problems or developmental opportunities need to be explored and resolved in the partnership? When will we do this?*

> ➤ *What do we think is going well? What is not going well . . .*

>> o *In the store? Why?*

>> o *In the partnership? Why?*

This recap conversation can occur at the conclusion of the store visit or later, either by phone or face-to-face.

## A CRITICAL WORD OF CAUTION

The transition from the defensive IDC approach to store visits to a developmental OID approach will likely mobilize store manager anxiety and defenses as a natural protective reflex to change. This is not necessarily all bad or counterproductive. Learning anxiety can be a powerful catalyst for change. Still, to ensure productive change, our recommended developmental conversations and store visit process require, first and foremost, a radical revision of the VP, DM and store manager roles and a corresponding radical revision of focus and intent.

The roles, in our view, must shift from those of auditor, compliance officer, and operator to executives and developers of leaders and teams. The focus of the VP needs to be on building and upgrading a high-performance DM team. Likewise, the focus of the DM needs to be on building and upgrading a high-performance district store management team and the focus of the store manager on building and upgrading a high-performance store team. The intentions must shift from taking control to fix the stores and save face and win at all costs, to collaboratively facilitating development through continuous partnering and learning.

These changes in role, focus, intention, and approach are difficult to realize. They require, as noted above, a developmental orientation to action and leadership and a corresponding productive indifference toward *presenting problems* in the store. This "productive indifference" doesn't mean that the field executive no longer cares about store conditions or actual results. On the contrary, the field executive remains actively concerned, but at a different level and with a very different focus.

To facilitate these changes, a type of action learning in the field must be employed to achieve necessary unlearning prior to new learning. One methodology for doing so is addressed in some detail in the Epilogue to this book, where we present our own approach to developing VPs and DMs in the field through Action Learning and Applied Action Science.

It will also be important for the DM to adequately inform the store manager of the changes that need to be made in his store visit process and the developmental purpose of such changes. How such informing occurs needs to be designed and tested carefully. In our experience, the optimal approach has involved the DM in one-on-one conversations with each store manager prior to the revised visit to provide the necessary background, context, and purpose of changes in the store visits. The rationale for change is provided in our research and conclusions as set forth in this book. Even more important are the executive's own reasons for change.

Many executives have tried to change their approach to field management without really confronting and challenging their own defensive orientation to action and competing commitments. Consequently, their attempted transition failed. For example, in the name of developmental inquiry, many leaders essentially enter into circular forms of soft interrogation, acting as a prosecuting attorney while treating the store manager as a hostile witness.

The name of the game in this counterfeit developmental approach is, again, simply to "get" the store manager to see the store through the field executive's eyes and to do what the field executive believes needs to be done to fix the store. This makes their process nothing more than the IDC approach disguised as a collaborative, developmental conversation. What's missing are a truly collaborative and developmental orientation and a true commitment to partnership and learning. What's missing is the Leadership Factor. Additionally, even the best intentioned attempts at change have met with derailing resistance because the necessary preparatory conversations did not happen effectively, or at all.

The required transition from the DOA to the COA and from the IDC Approach to the OID Approach cannot occur without rigorous external and internal coaching with coaches qualified and certified in the skills of Action Science as applied to the retail sector. Expert Action Science coaches function as necessary facilitators for the action research and design process, a process that requires "active (critical) observation" and creative collaboration.

## WHAT ABOUT STORES IN CRISIS?

Clearly in situations where the store is experiencing escalating operating expenses or declines in sales, profits, or other critical indicators, and when those negative declines are chronic or increasing at an accelerating rate, we need to stop the bleeding. So too, if the store team is in crisis as evidenced by rapid and substantial turnover, conflict or real insubordination. If, as an extreme example, a customer is shot in the store, as was actually the case in one company we worked with, and the store manager is panicking and doesn't know what to do, this would clearly not be an appropriate time to conduct a developmental conversation!

In such cases, taking immediate control is necessary to attend to the crisis and restore stability. Still, developmental opportunities are present and need to be returned to after the store is stabilized.

Emergency or crisis situations call for a different orientation to action, an orientation that is neither defensive nor collaborative and developmental in nature. Let's refer to it as the Survival Orientation to Action, or SOA. This orientation to action is based on the needs for rescue and turnaround, and the values for stability, order, and survival in the face of chronic, rapid downturn or crisis. Clearly the IDC approach would be indicated in such situations. Other necessary control-based interventions might also be required. Their approaches would vary but would be hands-on and directive in nature. Although the prescription of such approaches is beyond the scope of this book, the term "command and control" seems appropriately descriptive.

What's important to note here is that the SOA is acknowledged and accepted as being *temporary* and supersedes the COA *only* in times of genuine crises. After the turnaround is completed or the crisis is contained and the store management team has been rebuilt or upgraded as needed, the COA resumes its prominence as the primary orientation to action.

It's also important to note that the SOA also has its counterfeit version. The counterfeit SOA, which, as before, is the DOA in disguise, can be detected by the reasoning offered by the "in charge" executive for continuing to employ and persist with control-based approaches beyond apparent need.

What we need to realize and continually keep in mind is that the fundamental difference between the SOA or COA and the DOA, as between the actions of "inspect" and "observe" in the IDC and OID approaches respectively, is the *intent* of the leader. Our intentions essentially comprise our orientation to action as well as the nature of the action itself. This makes honesty to oneself of primary importance to leaders in their pursuit of consistent effectiveness.

## THE PROBLEM OF THE 'GOOD' PERFORMING STORE

We often tell our clients that we are just as concerned, if not more so, about their good performing stores as we are with their marginal or poor performing stores. Why is that? First, because in our experience too many good performing stores simply don't know why they're successful - what specifically accounts for their success - even though they think they do. This can compromise their ability to sustain their success. Second, because too many good performing stores, while exceeding plan and brand standards overall, are not achieving such success in every key result area of the business and don't know why. Third, because too many successful stores don't realize what strengths and dependencies make them vulnerable to reversal. Fourth, even if store teams know why they're successful and keep doing what makes them good, their best practices often block them from greater improvement and levels of performance. The governing value is to preserve the status quo, i.e. "keep up the good work," "keep doing what you're doing," and "if it isn't broken, don't fix it." After all, how can a "best practice" be any better? Hence, the 'good' becomes the enemy of the 'great.'

There are countless examples of good performing stores (and organizations) that unexpectedly fell from prominence for one or all of those reasons. Because of this, we recommend that as part of the DM's developmental agenda, the store managers of good performing stores be continually engaged in action research and *reflective learning* through the following questions:

- *What specific internal and external factors have caused or determined your success? How do we know that?*

- *What "best practices" have you implemented and how might the implementation of these practices undermine learning and delimit your continued success? How is the "good the enemy of the great" in this store? What's working that needs to be broken to design something better?*

- *Where are you vulnerable? What are you assuming about your success that might limit your understanding and vision of your vulnerability?*

- *How might yours and your team's strengths work against you and how are you managing this paradox? (Note: For an excellent treatment of the idea that our strengths are our weaknesses, see The Paradox of Success by John O'Neil (1994), published by Tarcher-Putnam.)*

- *What are your dependencies, i.e. what or who are you counting on that makes you vulnerable and how are you managing these dependencies?*

- *What goals, expectations, values, and beliefs might set you up for failure or derailment through defensive action and competing commitments?*

Our research has uncovered many instances of overall store performance being produced by a critical few team members, including the store manager or management team. These critical few carry a disproportionate load of the work and are relied on to compensate for the ineffective managers and non-producing associates in other departments. This 'muscling' of good performance is, in reality, a weakness, not strength. Nor is it a sign of strength for associate engagement to be based on loyalty to a charismatic or popular store manager, or on the best practices of high volume departments, or on the positive energy of past achievements, or on a favorable marketing mix of location, price and promotions.

While results are the ultimate measure of success, they do not solely define great store performance. What we look for is how consistently and effectively the store manager is applying the Leadership Factor in developing and upgrading his team as set forth in Chapter 3 and whether or not the store is making or exceeding plan in every category, or key result area.

## GREAT STORE PERFORMANCE AND THE DILEMMA OF CENTRALIZED STORE SUPPORT

Everything covered to this point has focused on creating great store performance through the effective placement and continual development of the store manager. The premise of the book has been that store manager performance is the highest-leverage problem and opportunity to store success and market advantage. And our related premise, as set forth in the Introduction, has been that great store performance requires the store manager to function as a General Manager with full P&L responsibilities and as a leader fully vested in the building and upgrading of his store team.

All this leads to one overarching question. For those retailers who understand that their stores are the only significant result producing assets of the company, that their stores are the first line of defense against the competition, and that great store performance is essential to sustained market advantage**... what *is* the _necessary_ role of the store manager?**

How empowered do store managers need to be? What responsibilities do they need to take on? What types of decisions do they need to make? What results do they need to deliver and how much autonomy do they need to have to deliver those results? Should they function as entrepreneurs and empowered GMs of multi-million dollar businesses with full P&L responsibility, or as cost center managers, operators or custodians? Accordingly, what is management willing to pay for? What power is it willing to release? These questions pertain to any role whose sole and primary stewardship is one or more stores.

The answers to these questions will significantly affect the roles of store support functions like marketing, merchandising, asset protection, human resources, and operations. In this final section we shift the focus from the store manager to the issue of store support and encourage field executives to open the field of dialogue by first considering, then raising and addressing the following critical questions: What does *store support* mean and look like when the store manager is truly empowered to run the store as its owner and GM? How would this meaning differ if the store manager's role were limited to that of an operator, supervisor and custodian? And how do the meanings shift as the role of the store manager is defined at different points between these two poles?

Currently in many retail organizations, store support functions drive the business and dictate policy, programs, systems, and controls to the stores. Store managers function more as cost center managers and operators than GMs, and are expected to comply with the dictates and requirements imposed by store support functions through the field chain of command.

In all the retail organizations we have worked with and researched over the years, the store managers, or directors, feel they have very limited power or authority to run their stores. To them the primary customers are their DM, the VP, store support directors and paying customers in that order. These store managers do not have a voice regarding what to sell, what price to sell it for, where or how to place and merchandise their products, what or how much to stock, what to promote, how to lay out their store space, what programs to accept or decline, or which managers or supervisors within their stores to hire or fire without the DM's approval. Nor do they have any control over the timing of changes or the number of new programs imposed upon them. Yet they are held accountable for store performance and results. Is there a possible problem here?

In support of this arrangement, many field executives and store support directors argue that store managers aren't qualified to make such decisions and that the region would never be able to determine best practices or achieve the necessary consistency, efficiencies, and economies of scale through decentralized store management and store support. This argument sounds reasonable and compelling, but is it?

Why can't the necessary efficiencies be realized though mechanisms other than strict centralization? Why couldn't they be created, for example, through a stores-driven infrastructure designed to preserve and enhance line integrity and the alignment of the stores and store support organizations through partnering? This possibility is somewhat elaborated on below.

Further, what are these field executives and store support leaders assuming regarding the possible (not current) role and qualifications of the empowered store manager? Or what are they assuming regarding the bases and requirements for competitive advantage? Or regarding available structural options? Or the likelihood of feared "anarchy" through controlled (not defensive) decentralization? Or the degree of control afforded by performance partnership agreements? Or, more personally, the nature and necessity of their own current roles and contribution?

Finally, what facts or evidence support such assumptions and what are the alternatives to the traditional conclusions reached? There's a tension here that needs to be addressed. Are store support directors mandating compliance to best practices without evaluating store fit and optimal execution at the store level? Is it possible that best practices are being adopted blindly by store support directors without critically analyzing what makes them work at particular stores?

There seems to be a tendency for store support directors to simply try to superimpose what worked at one or more test stores on other stores without accounting for variations in circumstances or demographics. Store managers and associates are essentially being told to do something that they really don't own. This can undermine personal commitment.

What about the ideas of consistency and conformity? Certainly store teams need to be in compliance with company policy, brand standards and safety regulations, and such compliance is not negotiable. But when consistency and conformity are espoused and enforced as supreme values, might there be a high corresponding risk of disenfranchising store managers from the leadership and the creativity that is needed to bring about true ownership and commitment?

Might the tight control of centralization, in fact, tend to dis-empower store managers and correspondingly undermine accountability by depriving them of the necessary autonomy and risk inherent in ownership? Are these companies creating a bureaucracy that hinders decision-making and makes store teams less responsive to the customer? Does a reliance on consistency and conformity undermine speed in responding to shifting market trends? Are these companies placing unnecessary encumbrances on the store manager preventing him from doing what he could be doing to make his store more profitable and customer focused? Are these policies breeding a culture of frustration, resistance, and defensiveness?

Our research in the field leads to only one answer to all of the above questions, and that answer is an unqualified "yes."

According to Block's vision of stewardship (See Chapter 3), store support directors would best function as 'suppliers' or 'bankers' to the store managers. In essence, the store support staff should be asking the store managers, as their expert advisors, suppliers, and bankers, what they need in order to get the results they're committed to deliver. "What kind of HR support do you need?" "What kind of market intelligence do you need?" "Systems support?" "Financial and accounting support?" "Marketing and merchandizing support?" The assumption that the store manager can't or shouldn't be involved in such business decisions because he or she is not qualified could be limiting, or even fatal to the pursuit of great store performance. Store managers don't have to be involved in data or idea generation, analysis and planning. But what stops the store support staff, for instance, from viewing the store manager as a "client" of support functions and viewing themselves as providers and suppliers of information, counsel, and resources?

This is not to say that the store manager must always know what information or advice he needs or when. Nor does this suggest that the store manager must be a specialist in all areas of store support. Quite the contrary. GMs by definition are not specialists. They are generalists. So, assuming professional, qualified store managers are in place functioning as GMs, what exactly are the concerns? The fact that the current base of store managers might not be capable of functioning as GMs is not relevant in a conversation about future possibilities. Besides, who is to say that all store managers currently in place are not capable of functioning as GMs? Such a possibility has never really been seriously put to the test and could not be as long as field executives and store support directors persist defensively in their own skilled incompetence.

Perhaps, on a more relevant level, there's a fear that if store support functions step aside and let the store managers run their store, the region, and ultimately, the company, will end up with thousands of different systems and policies that won't link with each other, or won't be able to purchase in bulk to offer lower prices, or won't present a consistent shopping experience or brand image.

Is such an argument justifiable or valid? What are the assumptions that these conclusions are based on and what are the facts that support such arguments? Why should reasonable people assume that a new breed of store executive, or even existing store managers, would be unreasonably resistant to good counsel based on valid and compelling information? And why should anyone assume that such feared unreasonableness or poor judgment could not be adequately anticipated and provided for in the PPA? Is it possible that the anxiety runs to a deeper, more personal level? Is there a fear that in classifying store support functions as suppliers to the store managers, the store support teams might lose organizational status, power and security?

We understand the importance of consistency, compliance and conformity to brand integrity. We understand the importance of centralized purchasing and systems and the cost efficiencies that come from related economies of scale. And we understand the competitive virtues and advantages of best practices. These are realities that need to be attended to in order for the business as a whole to be profitable and competitive.

However, acknowledging these realities does not change the importance of resolving the tension between these 'operational' values for consistency, conformity, and compliance, and the super-ordinate 'performance' values for empowerment, accountability, learning, and commitment that have to exist at the store level in order to create and sustain great store performance.

To begin to manage such tension, management needs to approach it through dialogue, rather than through edict, argument and debate. They need to recognize both the tension and its implications on store and company performance. They need to explore how they can honor both sets of values and manage the tension between the business realities that are governed by the operational values and the business realities that are governed by the performance values inherent in the three fundamentals of effective execution. This, we think, can best be accomplished by challenging beliefs, testing assumptions, discussing the undiscussable, balancing advocacy and inquiry, and exploring meaning to come to creative, new solutions.

There are certain operational guidelines and decision rights that are non-negotiable. There are business realities that pose non-negotiable constraints on management. But it is possible to honor the need for economies of scale, compliance, and consistency and also honor the needs of the store manager to own the business and be empowered. Where is that line drawn? This, it seems to us, is an important question.

Perhaps, as intimated above, store-wide decisions regarding those policies, programs, systems, and product contracts directly affecting the stores might best be influenced by rotating, demographically representative panels of store managers. At the program adoption level, these rotating GM line-panels would be informed of store-wide company and regional goals, strategies and opportunities, or proposed initiatives, and advised accordingly by regional store support directors. They would then make informed recommendations regarding the feasibility, adoption, adaptation, and execution of such proposed initiatives or opportunities to the Regional VP, who would then offer them, if necessary, to the next level of management in the context of company-wide goals, policies and strategies.

The line panel's input and recommendations would ultimately work their way up the (hopefully few) appropriate levels of management for revision and decision. The panel would be in the decision loop every step of the way by collaboratively engaging decision makers through ongoing advocacy and inquiry. At the execution level, other expert staff panels or change teams within the region might be charged with the staff work of communication, training, production, and contract negotiations. The move would be from hierarchy to partnership.

Let's look at an actual case. One retailer contracted with a major supplier of disposable diapers for a specific display to be placed in every store in return for certain volume discounts. Within one of its divisions, a particular store was located in a retirement community where there were no children. The store manager made the decision that to put a large, prominent diaper display in the entrance of the store as required would not only be ineffective, it would look bad to the customers – a bad decision all the way around. He wasn't going to sell many, if any, diapers and he was going to demonstrate to his customers that he was not in touch with the market. His decision was reversed by the Director of Marketing in that division who stated emphatically, "You will comply with the program because we agreed to it contractually."

Now here is a case where the store manager was powerless to make the best decision for his store. He was up against a non-negotiable reality based upon the product contract that was agreed to. But why did it have to be this way? This wasn't the only store in a market where such a program didn't make good business sense. There were others. So why wasn't a potential situation like this taken into consideration so that reasonable exceptions could be made down to a slightly lower level of compliance? Were the store managers informed of this opportunity and involved in the program adoption process or in the determination of terms and diaper loads?

How might this case, and numerous others like it, have been managed differently using divisional or regional line-panels comprised of a representative team of GM-level store managers as suggested above? What might have been the effect on the speed and quality of execution had the integrity of the line organization been kept intact? What might have been the effect on the quality of decision-making and execution had the staff store support and line stores organizations collaborated effectively as partners through a more representative infrastructure?

Clearly, through greater collaboration, a level of flexibility could have been built into this program that would have allowed the store managers, with help from their advisors, to optimize both company and store results in relation to established goals and objectives. We think it's possible to create market advantage when store support functions and stores are operating as partners from the COA instead of the DOA.

In our experience, existing business realities are so often approached with such a single-minded agenda that management fails to explore its own inferences and the possibilities that might arise through a wider form of dialogue and collaboration. Management essentially fails to distinguish what is truly non-negotiable vs. what it *makes* non-negotiable through its own assumptions and defensive reasoning. The results? Usually tighter controls, less empowerment, and compromised performance.

So where might we begin? Perhaps the best place to begin is with robust dialogue around a few profound and provocative questions. The questions below are offered as a start. Ask yourselves as a management team:

- *What does the vision of 'great store performance' mean to us?*

- *What are the implications of the roles and functions of 'store manager' and 'store support' on great store performance?*

- *What does the desired role (or 'stewardship') of the store manager look like in terms of responsibilities, decision-types and rights, expected results and operational guidelines?*

- *What does 'store support' mean in relation to great store performance as defined?*

- *How do store support functions best "support" qualified, empowered and accountable store managers?*

- *What is the stewardship of each Store Support function?*

- *What are the principles and values that govern the partnership between stores and the store support organization? How might the ideas of 'support' and 'stewardship' inspire and influence such principles and values?*

- *What structural alternatives might be possible and preferable in achieving the best of both centralized and decentralized worlds?*

- *Specifically, in relation to the question above, how might we create a more dynamic 'partnering' structure that enhances and maintains 'line' integrity and 'line/staff' alignment for improved store performance and accountability?*

- *How would such a structure translate to actual PPAs between stores and store support functions?*

Participating in such dialogue sessions does not involve debate. Dialogue, as a unique form of communication, is an inquiry into meaning and diverse perspectives and beliefs. It also includes an inquiry into the facts supporting such perspectives and beliefs. Through dialogue, individuals are invited to listen to themselves as well as to others, actively and respectfully. Additionally, participants are invited and urged to explore their own and others' thinking, suspend their judgments and reactions, and open their minds to different points of view. Expertly facilitated dialogue sessions can be powerful ways to transform rigid polarization ('either/or') into a more inclusive polarity ('both/and') within the organization, and we suggest it begin at the senior management level within the Region or Division. (Note: The theory and practice of dialogue is covered very well in the book *Dialogue: The Art of Thinking Together* by William Isaacs (1999), published by Currency-Doubleday.)

The stores are the key result producing areas of business. The store support functions do not directly interface with the paying customer or produce financial results. The stores do. This is a basic reality of the business. Unfortunately, in too many retail organizations, the store support functions see themselves as, and are considered to be, responsible for generating store results based upon what they've done to define all the programs that take place in a store. This "tail wagging the dog" phenomenon is, in our judgment, compromising store performance and results and making the notion of store support an absurd contradiction in terms. We think there's a better option.

## CONCLUSION

The alternative to the Defensive Orientation to Action (DOA), which, as we learned in the last chapter, explains the third dilemma regarding why we persist in doing what doesn't work (Chapter 4), is the Collaborative Orientation to Action (COA). The DOA is primary, deeply ingrained in all of us and defensive in nature, resulting in control-based approaches to action and interaction with others. The alternative orientation to action is developmental in nature according to the vision of development presented in the third chapter.

Both alternative orientations, or transcendent (i.e. Meta) theories of action, are based on a discrete set of core values and action strategies, and the transition from the DOA to the COA (chapters 4 and 5 respectively), and consequently from inconsistent store performance to world-class store performance, is difficult and arduous to say the least. In our experience, such a transition is a slow, laborious process involving one developmental conversation at a time.

Hopefully we have adequately shown that the pursuit of great store performance will remain an illusion if retail field executives continue to focus on the wrong problems (Chapter 2), omit the Leadership Factor

(Chapter 3), and persist unnecessarily in their control-based approaches to field management (Chapter 1). Also, great store performance will remain an illusion if field and store support executives continue to persist in defensively motivated, control-based store support (Chapter 5), if store managers continue to function as operators instead of stewards or owners of their business, and if management continues to chase the 'quick fix' through the acceptance and advancement of flawed advice and the employment of counterfeit developmental programs (Chapters 4 and 5).

For leaders who are truly committed to the creation of great store performance, there is no quick or easy path. The developmental strategy we advocate in this book is just that, a significant, long-term strategic initiative that we insist must start at the very top of the store's organization with the CEO's understanding and support and the senior stores executive's support and participation. This is a strategy that will not only transform store performance, but will facilitate sustained cultural change.

# KEY INSIGHTS FROM CHAPTER 5:

➤ *The alternative to the Defensive Orientation to Action (DOA) is the Collaborative Orientation to Action (COA).*

➤ *To ensure great store performance, field executives need to transition from the DOA to the COA by adopting and applying the Observe/Inquire/Develop (O/I/D) approach to store visits instead of the prevailing Inspect/Direct/Correct (IDC) approach.*

➤ *The OID approach is applied through a new developmental store visit process that focuses on the application of the Leadership Factor and the development and upgrading of store managers through ongoing partnering, accountability, and learning conversations.*

➤ *Stores in crisis should be stabilized before engaging in long-term development efforts. This requires a Survival Orientation to Action (SOA) which is not the same as the DOA, and which is temporary and subsequently transitions to the COA after the turnaround has been accomplished and the store management team has been rebuilt and upgraded.*

➤ *Good performing stores present a unique challenge of their own, requiring field executives to work collaboratively with the store managers of such stores to discover, explore, and effectively attend to the various vulnerabilities that could contribute to reversal and downfall.*

➤ *The tensions between store support functions and the stores need to be productively resolved before great store performance can occur. Great store performance requires fully empowered store managers, functioning as partners or stewards and GMs of their business, and store support professionals functioning as suppliers and advisors.*

# APPENDIX A:

# GUIDELINES FOR EFFECTIVE INQUIRY

| Do | | Don't |
|---|---|---|
| Provide a developmental context at the beginning of the visit. | | Leave it to others to figure out what you're doing or why. |
| Pursue a well thought–out line of questioning. | | Question in circles. |
| Use open-ended questions starting with: What, how, when, who, where, why. | | Ask leading questions to get them to your thinking. |
| Take your time. Slow down the conversation to listen, confirm and reflect. | | Rush or push with your questions. Ask rapid fire questions. |
| Listen critically and with respect to understand. Let them answer. | | Listen to reply. Interrupt. Cut them off. |
| Engage them and be present when they speak or answer. Look at them and listen deeply. | | Look away, walk way or lose connection. |

| | | |
|---|---|---|
| Ask for meanings and explanations in response to vague, general, tentative, evasive, elusive answers. | | Gloss over non-answers to go to different topics or areas of concern. |
| Ask in the attitude of curiosity for mutual discovery and exploration. | | Ask to entrap, lead, control or manipulate the conversation. |

# APPENDIX B:

# REFLECTIVE, RESEARCH AND DESIGN-BASED LEARNING INTERVENTION: PERSPECTIVE

The *reflective learning intervention* is a COA action strategy that is developmental in intent, resulting in greater empowerment, accountability, and internal commitment. This intervention is interactive and collaborative in nature and takes the form of a crucial, if not difficult, conversation that can be at once illuminating and energizing as well as discomforting.

The focus of the Learning Intervention is not on downloading information, training, or providing feedback or direction. Nor is it on the technique of asking probing questions, as in conducting an interview, performance evaluation or interrogation. Learning interventions are not exercises in manipulation, direction or control. You are not trying to get the other person to think or act in a certain way or buy in to your way of thinking or acting. These conversations, or collaborations, are designed to facilitate development, greater internal commitment, and ownership through more reflective and productive action.

In this regard, the following model, instructions, and related conversational process are important to follow.

## REFLECTIVE LEARNING INTERVENTION MODEL:

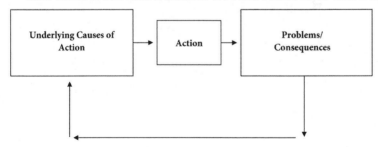

# REFLECTIVE LEARNING INTERVENTION SCHEMATIC

## PART I: FACILITATE UNLEARNING (Problem is recurring and action has taken place.)

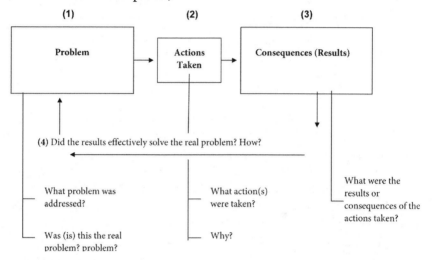

## PART II: FACILITATE NEW LEARNING (Problem that needs to be addressed. No action has been taken.)

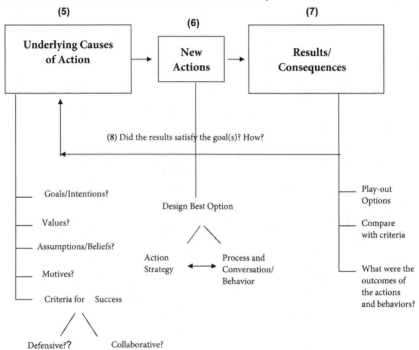

## REFLECTIVE LEARNING PROCESS: GENERAL INSTRUCTIONS

- *In working with the reflective learning process below, keep the reflective learning model above in mind, maintain an attitude of curiosity, listen actively, and critically and participate collaboratively, subjecting all shared and stated thoughts, ideas and concerns, assertions, or opinions to appropriate inquiry.*

- *The model itself, as well as the corresponding process below, is useful and productive as the underlying structure of the learning conversation, serving as the necessary scaffolding upon which to build the conversation.*

- *Finally, it is crucial to approach learning or developmental conversations from a COA mind-set, with a practiced commitment to the values of:*

  *(1) producing valid information.*

  *(2) free, informed choice.*

  *(3) internal commitment through researched actions, mutual, creative collaboration and personal success.*

- *Follow the process below carefully, utilizing horizontal inquiry as you move through discovery from step to step, and vertical inquiry as you explore and analyze more deeply the other's goals, intentions, thoughts, suggestions, opinions and underlying reasons, meanings, assumptions and beliefs. Throughout the conversations, you may participate collaboratively, sharing your own thoughts, ideas, and conclusions while balancing inquiry and advocacy by making your thinking visible and inviting the other to explore and challenge, through inquiry, your thinking and ideas as well as their own.*

  o *Note: In the beginning of your attempt to facilitate the transition from the DOA to the COA, it is advisable to share your thoughts, ideas or opinions sparingly so as not to prematurely abort the other's thinking.*

Following these instructions and the process below, your conversation will naturally proceed, as illustrated on page 314 on a continuum from discovery to exploration to analysis and finally to closure as you utilize both horizontal and vertical inquiry and collaborate creatively while balancing inquiry and advocacy.

## REFLECTIVE LEARNING PROCESS
## (RELATE THE STEPS BELOW TO THE REFLECTIVE
## LEARNING MODEL)

1. *Discover and explore, through observation and inquiry, the nature (i.e. low-leverage problem (LLP) or high-leverage problem (HLP)), duration and causes of the presenting problem, or dilemma, including*

the needs for simple training, process improvement, and performance corrections and enhancement.

2. Discover and explore through observation and inquiry, what, if anything was done to resolve the problem and why.

3. Determine through observation and inquiry the actual results of any action(s) taken.

4. Confirm whether of not, from the actor's perspective, the actual outcome of the action(s) taken satisfied the actor's goals and intentions and why, or why not. (Note: At this point, if it is determined that this is a LLP requiring simple training in the form of suggesting/showing/ observing/correcting, then proceed accordingly with training and move on to the next challenge or opportunity. If, however, it is determined in steps 1-4 that this is a HLP, then proceed to step 5 with reflective learning.)

5. Determine, through inquiry, the underlying causes of action. Test for validity the actor's beliefs and assumptions about the nature and cause of the problem and explore how the goals, intentions, and purposes of the necessary intervention or action to be taken might need to change to produce necessary information and enable effective choice and action. Also, establish, through collaboration and analysis, the evaluative criteria for selecting the best approach, or action to be taken, in ultimately resolving the problem or attending to the need.

6. Generate, through brainstorming, possible options as alternative approaches, and work together to select and design the best option, along with corresponding action strategies and behaviors congruent with the established goals and intentions. In reducing the action strategies to observable behavior you might ask:

   (A) What would/could you do (or how would/could you approach this)? Then what? What else?

   (B) How did you arrive at these strategies? What was your thinking?

   (C) What would this look like behaviorally? How would this conversation play out?

7.  *Examine and evaluate together, through analysis and role-play, the likely outcome(s) of the designed option.*

8.  *Explore together, through observation and inquiry, the likely consequences or outcomes of the designed approach in light of established goals and criteria for success as established in step #5 above and modify the design accordingly. Come to closure on the best design and explore how and when this new theory of action will be tried and tested in the workplace. (Note: Steps 1-4 in this process work toward unlearning, while steps 5-8 work toward new learning, internal commitment, and accountability through the creating of new, more effective approaches, or theories of action.)*

## POSSIBLE QUESTIONS TO BE USED IN INQUIRY

| Process Reference | Horizontal Inquiry | Vertical Inquiry |
|---|---|---|
| Step 1 | • What is the problem as you see it?<br><br>• What might be causing this problem? | • Why is that a problem? What does (X,Y) mean to you?<br>• How so? What else? What would that assume? Why? Why not? |
| Step 2 | • Is this a recurring problem?<br><br><br><br>• What was (has been) done to correct this problem? | • How long has it been a problem? When did you first become aware of it? When did you first take action? Why not sooner (if applicable)?<br>• What does that mean? What did that look like? Why that action (or inaction)? What did that assume? What was the goal? Intention? Motivation? Strategy? Why? |

| Step 3 | • What did your approach accomplish? | • How do you account for (or explain) the results? What else? How so? What does that mean?  Assume? |
| | • What were the consequences of your action on behavior? | • What does that mean? What did that look like? How do you know that? What don't you know? |
| | | • (Same as above) |
| | • What were the consequences of your action on learning/development? | |
| Step 4 | • What was your goal?<br>• What did you want to accomplish by taking this action? | • Why that goal?<br>• Why was this important? What did this goal assume? |
| | • Did you accomplish your goal? | • How do you know? What did success look like? What does that mean? Assume? |

| Step 5 | • What might you be assuming or believing (about the problem itself, the risks involved, your own ability, your manager, others, etc.) that might influence the way you approach this problem? | • How valid is this belief or assumption? How do you know? What don't you know that you might need to know to either confirm or disconfirm this belief or assumption? How can you come to know this, i.e. what information would you need to produce and what would make such information valid or reliable? |
| --- | --- | --- |
| | • What do you want to accomplish? What are your intentions moving forward? | • Why is that important? How is that relevant to the problem at hand? How might this goal or intention influence your action? What's the upside of achieving this goal? What's the possible downside? |
| | • How would your goals and intentions need to change to enable you to make the best decisions with respect to how to best address this problem? | • What difference do you think that change might make? How so? What about...? |
| | • What will success look like? What are the criteria for determining success in this situation? | • Why? What else? How so? What does that mean? Look like? |

| Step 6 | • What could be done differently in resolving this problem? How would this play out (or look) behaviorally? | • What else? Why? What does that assume? How did you arrive at that? What would that look like? |
|---|---|---|
| Step 7 | • How does this option stand up under scrutiny?<br>• What is the upside? Downside?<br>• What criteria does it satisfy? What are the misses?<br>• What are the implications on…?<br>• How is this option/approach different/similar to other options/approaches tried and considered?<br>• Why this option instead of…?<br>• How might this (selected) option be tested? | • How so? Why? Why not? How did you to that conclusion?<br>• What does that mean?<br>• What does that assume?<br>• What else?<br>• In what way(s) |

| Step 8 | • What is the likely outcome? | • What would that look like? |
|---|---|---|
| | • Would it satisfy the goal? | • How so? |
| | • What in your approach can be confirmed? Disconfirmed? | • How so? How do you know that? Why is that? |
| | • What might the consequences on behavior be? (how might the other react)? | • What would that look like? What would that assume? |
| | • What might the consequences be on learning? | • What would that look like? |
| | • What would the resulting conversation look like? | • How will you test its effectiveness? |

## DEVELOPMENTAL CONVERSATION CONTINUUM

| Discovery $\longrightarrow$ | Exploration $\longrightarrow$ | Analysis $\longrightarrow$ | Closure |
|---|---|---|---|
| Variance/ Presenting Problem | Options | Control or Collaboration? | Make Decision |
| Root Cause(s) | Criteria for Evaluation | Satisfaction of Criteria? | Plan Action |
| | Underlying Causes (goals, values, beliefs, assumptions, motives) | Test Results of New Approach | Take Action |
| | Appropriate Tests | | |
| | Defensive Routines/ Behavior | | |

**RESULTS OF ACTION TAKEN**

# APPENDIX C:

# ALTERNATIVE DEVELOPMENTAL STORE VISIT PROCESS

## PERSPECTIVE:

- *The nature of all store visits is developmental, with the overarching objective of improving and sustaining performance and results through the creation of learning, high performing, empowered store managers and store teams. Accordingly, the focus of the store visit is not the condition of the store, but the development of the store manager and other managers. You are not really visiting stores, you're visiting store managers.*

- *Underneath every presenting store problem is a store team problem, and underneath every persistent, recurring execution problem is a store manager problem.*

- *The entire store manager visit might take six or more hours (for all stage visits) and is very developmental in nature. It cannot be rushed.*

- *The key to effective store manager visits is preparation. You need to study and know the store's performance numbers and other necessary background information before visiting the store to provide a necessary context for development.*

- *Not all three stages, or developmental conversations, need to be completed in a single visit on a single day. More than one day might be needed to complete all three stages. The "recap" needs to occur at the end of the each stage of the visit.*

  o *Note: In the beginning, it might be advisable to begin with a lengthy stage three visit to first empower the store manager and then discover, explore and analyze what the store manager is doing (or not doing) regarding the three fundamentals of effective execution, i.e. empowerment, development, and accountability with his/her team.*

- *The operating mechanism for all three stages is the design-based learning intervention.*

## PRE-VISIT CONVERSATION WITH STORE MANAGER

- *Present the purpose of the visit and how it differs from the purpose of prior visits and why.*

- *Specify what will not happen in the visit.*

- *Specify what will happen (what will be different):*

  o *Briefly outline stages 1, 2 and 3.*

  o *Ask for questions.*

- *Pre-visit assignment:*

  o *Stage 1: Three operational problems the store manager is currently struggling with.*

  o *Stage 2: Store manager makes sure all managers are there for this stage.*

  o *Stage 3: Three significant developmental opportunities for each of his/her direct reports.*

- *Specify where the visit will take place and how long it will take.*

# DEVELOPMENTAL STORE VISITS (SCHEMATIC)

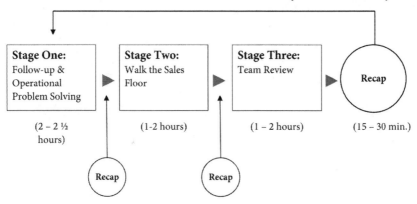

## STAGE ONE CONVERSATION
### FOLLOW-UP AND PROBLEM SOLVING

*Meet privately with the store manager and other managers, if appropriate.*

The purpose of this stage is to develop the store manager's ability to more effectively identify and solve process related operational problems.

1) *Follow up on previous learnings and ask for an accounting of operational performance in areas of concern.*

2) *Identify the store manager's top three concerns/problems and work with the store manager to effectively solve his/her top concern by facilitating problem solving through design-based learning.*

3) *Reveal your top operational concern(s) with the store manager based on your review of the numbers and knowledge of store performance and work with the store manager to effectively resolve your top concern or problem by facilitating problem solving with them through double-loop learning.*

## STAGE TWO CONVERSATION
### WALK THE FLOOR

In walking the floor with the store manager and department managers you will:

1) *Determine how the store manager and other managers walk the floor to improve store conditions.*

2) *Determine the extent to which the store manager and other managers are effectively identifying and solving operational and customer service problems on the sales floor.*

3) *Assess each department's goals, plans, and team readiness for optimizing sales.*

The purpose of this stage is to identify developmental opportunities regarding the store manager's ability to improve and maintain store conditions and sales performance through the development/empowerment of his/her team.

1) *Ask the store manager to walk the sales floor, department by department, with the department managers.*

   - *Note observations made, correctives taken and opportunities missed. Observe only. Do not offer correctives or direction.*

2) *Identify patterns and interactive dynamics. How did the store manager walk the floor? What approach did he/she use? What did he see? What did he miss? What was left unknown that was important for the store manager to know about the department manager's skill, ability, desire, perspective, management ability, team conditions, etc?*

3) *After the store manager completes the walk-through in each department, you may want to ask the store manager to engage other (department) managers directly in a conversation about their goals, plans, and team readiness for sales optimization and customer service.*

   *Possible questions:*

   - *What's your goal for increasing sales/customer service? Why this goal?*

- *What's your plan? How did you arrive at this plan? What actions does it call for? Why this (or that) action? Other options?*

- *Who else knows this plan besides you? (Ask a team member.) Does everyone in your department know what's expected of them? How would they know? (Test it.)*

4) *At the end of the walk-through, ask the store manager to recap the walk-through, beginning with store conditions and ending with department readiness to optimize sales and customer service. Then engage the store manager in design-based learning to develop a more effective approach to walking the sales floor.*

## STAGE THREE CONVERSATION
## TEAM REVIEW

Meet privately and preferably off-site with the store manager to explore team performance issues and concerns. This stage needs to be done in **every** visit. In many ways, this stage will be a natural outgrowth of stages one and two, since, at the heart of every operational problem and sales opportunity is a performance opportunity requiring team development and performance management. The purpose of this stage is to develop the store manager's ability to empower, develop and upgrade his/her team for better and more consistent execution and results.

1) *In this visit or conversation, it is recommended that the three fundamentals of effective execution be explored and taught to establish a necessary leadership foundation as soon as possible. For this reason, it is advisable to make this emphasis with the first visit. During this initial stage three visit, first discover and explore what the store manager knows, means, and understands with respect to the three fundamentals of effective execution. This is best accomplished through inquiry.*

2) *As you discover together the store manager's limits of understanding, prompt or prime further exploration by sharing ideas and exploring thoughts and reactions. Ultimately, a baseline understanding of these three fundamentals is essential and can be*

*established through teaching, modeling and example. Either way, your understanding of meaning must be clear enough to guide, teach and illustrate.*

3) *After establishing a baseline shared understanding and vision of these fundamentals, proceed to evaluate together whether or not the store manager is, in fact, empowering, developing, and holding his/her team accountable given the new understandings. Use these realizations to explore with the store manager how he/she would go about implementing the three fundamentals with his/her team:*

- *In subsequent stage three visits, explore performance concerns and what the store manager is doing (or not doing) to empower, develop, and foster accountability.*

- *Explore the store manager's difficulty or reluctance in dealing with personnel problems and in upgrading his/her team.*

## OPERATING MECHANISM
Design-Based Learning Intervention

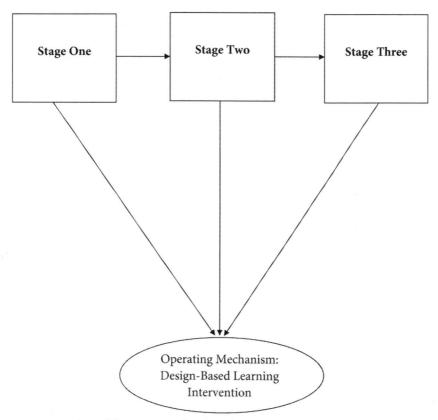

Design-based learning is fundamental to all three stages. Whatever dilemma comes out of each visit or stage can be facilitated and worked through using the design-based learning intervention model.

## RECAP
## CONDUCT A RECAP AFTER EACH STAGE

The purpose of the recap is to discover what learnings have occurred and to establish the basis of accountability and follow through. It will be both verbal and written.

- *What did you learn from our conversations today about...*

    a) *your store?*

    b)  *your team?*

    c)  *you?*

- *What opportunities (problems) will you explore (solve) with your team? How will you do that? When?*

- *What do you think you're doing well? Why?*

- *Where do you feel you need improvement? Why?*

- *What will you need to do (or do differently) to make such improvements/changes? What do your actions assume?*

You may ask the store manager to email you his/her response to the questions on the follow-up sheet. Continue the conversation by phone and/or email pursuing further inquiry as needed.

# EPILOGUE:

# CLOSING THOUGHTS AND GENERAL METHODOLOGY

Before presenting an overview of our general methodology in working with retail organizations, it might be instructive to address three possible reactions that we encounter at times in our conversations with other senior executives regarding our involvement in working with their VPs and DMs in improving store performance and results.

One reaction involves timing, and usually points to other internal development or strategic initiatives currently anticipated or in progress. There is a concern that there might be a conflict in emphasis or a distraction through the field coaching we do with VPs and DMs in the stores. This concern is understandable given certain assumptions held, but unnecessary and invalid given the facts.

Our work does not conflict with existing or new development or other strategic initiatives of an organization. The coaching is non-specific in terms of content and focuses on improving execution, accountability, and results through more enhancing performance and problem solving. This is not to say, however, that conflicts do not ever exist. Clearly, if your organization has embarked on a program that is based on, or would perpetuate, a "defensive orientation to action," there would be a disconnect.

A second reaction involves "overload," and usually points to how overwhelmed the VPs and DMs already are in terms of what is required of them, and thus there is a corresponding reluctance to burden them with one more thing to do that might, again, distract them from their strategic focus.

In response to this reaction, it is important to understand that we don't take executives away from their work. Rather we work with them while they are doing it. We observe the VPs and DMs doing their work and then, between and after store visits, we work with them to assess their performance, identify what is not working well, and collaborate with them to design and test more effective and more developmental problem-solving interventions in the stores with the store managers.

The concern about timing related to overload can be perhaps best addressed by questioning when the timing might be better. When will the

VPs and DMs ever *not* be overwhelmed, particularly, as the research shows, when the way they are managing in the field is creating many if not most of the problems that are overwhelming them? The action research is clear that the issue of time is a red herring. Their time problems are not about the management (or mismanagement) of time but rather about the way they are addressing problems in the stores.

As for the best time to do this, it's again important to refer to the nature of our work. In fact, while our involvement at any time of the year is appropriate, the best times for our coaches to be in the field with your executives are just before, during, and right after peak sales seasons when VPs and DMs are under the greatest pressure and are *most* overwhelmed. It's during these high-pressure seasons that we are able to see field executives at their most reactive and to observe their actual management approaches in the field with the greatest degree of accuracy and the greatest likelihood for unlearning and new learning.

The third reaction is perhaps most perplexing to us. After considering the merits of our work, some executives and HR professionals have expressed a concern that their field executives and store managers won't "get it" because the ideas expressed here are over their heads or would be too difficult for them to understand and apply. The assertion is that these field executives and store managers are not sufficiently educated or will resist anything that will require them to think too much, or to change their ways.

This reaction has no basis in fact. More complex versions of the content contained in this book have been received, understood, and applied enthusiastically by numerous field executives and store managers in various major retailers we have worked with over the years.

Granted, the changes called for in this book are not easy, and we have admitted as much. But the idea that such development is intellectually beyond the reach of retail field executives and store managers is again, from our perspective, completely baseless.

We regard our involvement as being strategic in nature. We are not offering yet another training program. (One of our clients suggested that, in the vernacular of Jim Collins, we provide a "technology accelerator" for moving the "fly wheel" of performance from "Good to Great.") Ours is a developmental coaching technology that improves execution through partnering and learning interventions in the field. While we value our partnerships with HR and the people functions within the organization, our work needs to be understood, appreciated, and positioned as a strategic development initiative. Otherwise it will likely not take root.

With all this said, we can proceed to our general methodology in working with our clients. Our engagements, of course, vary according to the needs of our clients, but the general framework presented below remains valid and relevant in most cases.

## DEVELOPMENT PROCESS (METHODOLOGY)

The details of our involvement vary depending on the structure of the field organization and the scope of involvement desired by the client. In the **first stage** of our involvement, we are usually retained to work with the EVP (or SVP) of stores and all the VPs. The various components of engagement in these traditional structures are as follows:

- *Field Coach obtains company orientation through initial interview(s) and the review of relevant information regarding store performance, i.e. strategies, objectives, assessments, metrics, standards and required core competencies and processes.*

- *Orientation meeting with Field Coach, EVP of stores and the VPs to break the ice, go over the process and answer questions.*

- *Assessment (2 levels):*

  - ✓ *Level One: Field Coach meets with each VP separately to obtain an understanding of their role and their vision of and 'espoused' approach to field leadership.*

  - ✓ *Level Two: Field Coach observes each VP and DM in the field as they visit with two stores in one of their most challenged districts to observe and assess their 'actual' approach.*

- *After assessing the VPs' and DMs' approach by observing them in action, the Field Coach meets with each VP for one day per month of field training and coaching over a six month period. Each VP receives six days of field coaching over a six month period where he will discover how his own management approach is undermining his best intentions and sub-optimizing store performance and results, and learn the new model of field leadership referred to earlier. (It should be noted here the new model of field leadership is the Observe/Inquire/ Develop (OID) Approach presented in chapter 5.) This model and methodology of field leadership we advocate and utilize ensures that the leadership competencies, core strategies, values, and standards of performance required by the organization are more deeply learned and applied in the field.*

In addition to the six days of field training and coaching for each VP, the EVP of stores will also be engaged by attending at least one day of field coaching in each region with the VP to learn and observe the process and the underlying theory in practice.

## EVALUATION

Regional performance is monitored and evaluated by the client during the first year of development and beyond using existing standard performance metrics. The Field Coach talks with the EVP of stores at three months and six months to review the overall progress of the process to ensure that the EVP is kept abreast of the progress in the field.

Finally, after the sixth monthly coaching session, the Field Coach will meet with the EVP of Stores and all the VPs to debrief the process, report learnings, receive and provide feedback, and determine next steps as indicated and desired. (Note: Field Coaches do not, as a matter of course, evaluate VP or DM performance on an individual basis with the VP or other VPs of HR and OD. Their performance will be self-evident through metrics and observation without the Field Coach's input, and it is crucial to the success of the process that the VPs and DMs see the Coach as their personal executive coach and not as the eyes and ears of their supervisor.)

## EXPECTED OUTCOMES

This field coaching process, which is expanded to include two or three other stages of development, is designed to ensure a deep level of executive development in the field of action science as it applies specifically to the retail industry, as well as field leadership development and consistent store performance and results. At the conclusion of the six month VP field coaching process, participants will:

* *Understand how their practiced, skilled routines and processes of leadership ensure that they will not solve problems at the right level or get the consistent results they want and need.*

* *Understand why store performance is so erratic and inconsistent.*

- *Understand the crucial differences among the DOA, COA, and SOA, and the implications of each orientation to action on great store performance.*

- *Learn how to facilitate personal change, development, and performance improvement through partnering and reflective, design-based learning interventions.*

- *Learn how to make the transition from the traditional inspect/direct/correct approach to retail field management (which results in compliance, problem recurrence, dependency, and the abdication of responsibility) to the observe, inquire and develop approach that results in greater commitment, independent thinking, empowerment, accountability, and more consistently effective performance and results.*

- *Learn how to develop leadership capability through the effective application of the Leadership Factor.*

In our experience, the initial focus on VP development seems preferred and indicated in light of the organizational and process dynamics involved in most retail organizations. The development of district managers and store managers is greatly leveraged through the development of the VPs first.

The **second stage** of development involves a three day Action Science workshop for DMs that explores their existing approaches to field management, problem solving, and store visits, and establishes a common base of understanding about the application of Action Science and the Leadership Factor in their work with store managers and the peer coaching work they will do with each other to foster and reinforce continued learning and development in the field.

This workshop is designed very differently from traditional training programs in that its focus is on actual performance problems in the field and on the necessary un-learning that must precede new learning for consistently effective problem solving and action to occur. It is recommended that these DM workshops be attended by functional store support directors in the region as well as the VP and be accompanied by field coaching and peer coaching.

The **third stage** of development involves the appointment and certification of one or more dedicated Action Science field coaches and facilitators for each region or division. The certification process involves additional training in the skills of Action Science and field training with an assigned field coach from our firm who has been working with the VPs and DMs to date. This stage of development is essential in building your internal capability to provide expert coaching and PPA facilitation beyond the level of peer coaching. It is recommended that the VPs attend the coach training with their designated coach candidates as well as provide backup candidates to enhance bench strength.

Finally, **a fourth possible stage** of development would involve six, one day coaching retreats for store managers. This stage is designed to accelerate and deepen the development effort by engaging the store managers in the process of unlearning counterproductive approaches and management practices and learning how to more effectively deal with performance/execution problems and build high-performance store teams through the application of the Leadership Factor. These one day workshops are likewise designed to facilitate action-based learning toward the assessment and design of more productive approaches in dealing with real time dilemmas or problems in their stores.

All four stages of development can span over a three to five year period and not every client uses all four stages. We recommend that a client begin with the first stage, which is the coaching of the VPs and DMs in the field and then naturally progress to stages two and three. These first three stages will likely span over two to three years and you should be able to continue the work internally thereafter.

## ABOUT THE AUTHOR

The Author's industry expertise spans the retail, pharmaceutical and high-technology sectors. Over the past nearly two decades of his career, Mr. Riskas has conducted pioneering work in the retail sector, conducting extensive action research in the area of field management practices and designing coaching and development interventions to help field executives consistently improve store performance, execution and results through applied Action Science. Some of the major retail companies the Author has worked with include Target Stores, Mervyn's, PetSmart, Dayton's, Hudson's, Office-Max, and Albertsons.

## FOR FURTHER INFORMATION

Questions or feedback concerning this book, as well as inquiries regarding consultation, action research and developmental field coaching services may be directed to the Author by mail, phone, fax or email

## CONTACT INFORMATION

Thomas Riskas
9030 West Sahara Avenue, Suite 462
Las Vegas, Nevada 89117

702-360-6797 (Direct Line)
702-360-8752 (Facsimile)
tjriskas @riskasassoc.com